A SPIRITUAL REBEL'S MANIFESTO

Climb Aboard
The Noah's Ark of
Consciousness

OTHER BOOKS BY JOHN HOGUE

Nostradamus: The Complete Prophecies
1000 for 2000 Startling Predictions for the New Millennium
Nostradamus: The New Millennium
The Last Pope "Revisited"
The Essential Nostradamus
Nostradamus: A Life and Myth
(ScryFy Short Story) Kamikaze Tomorrowland

A SPIRITUAL REBEL'S MANIFESTO

Climb Aboard
The Noah's Ark of
Consciousness

JOHN HOGUE

A SPIRITUAL REBEL'S MANIFESTO
Climb Aboard the Noah's Ark of Consciousness
Published by John Hogue
Copyright © 26 November 2017 by HogueProphecy
Publishing

Cover: John Hogue, Gail LaForest

ISBN: 978-1-387-46212-4

DEDICATION
To Diana Paxon and Melodi Lammond-Grundy.
An answer to their question: When does the Crazy Stop?

ACKNOWLEDGMENTS

Thanks to my conceptual editor, Francis Perry, my copy and proofing editor, Gail LaForest, and thanks to Vipassana: a mother *once* and a meditation *now*, in *oneness*.

TABLE OF CONTENTS

FOREWORD
When Does the Crazy Stop?

This book is the answer to a fundamental question posed by author Diana Paxon and shared in the following letter from my dear friend Melodi Lammond-Grundy.

***

My friend and mentor Diana Paxon was with me on the trip. She writes both fiction and various metaphysical "how too" books (mostly Asatru, runes, trance etc.).

She said she had noticed there seemed to be "something in the air or the planets or something that is making people act crazy on all levels, especially internationally but also personally."

I did my best without any documentation handy to explain your Oracle's views and Nostradamus (via your information) but I don't think I did a great job.

But she did have a great question she asked me to pass on and you have permission to use it…if you like.

Her question was; "Ask your friend John, When does the Crazy Stop?"

Now she's older than us so she doesn't mean in general, there is always "something" going on but she means this general mood of insanity in the personal, political and even planetary worlds (we spent a lot of time in Alpine villages trying to get phone signals to get updates on the fires in Northern California near where she lives).

I said I knew this was one "Window" for a great war with the US and Russia and another was in the 2020's and if we got past both then Edgar Cayce's future of no Third World War might kick in but I didn't have all the details.

Anyway, is there a way to answer her question in brief? If so she would much appreciate it and given the questions from the Germans, Brits, Swiss and Swedes at the conference I was just at on "Inclusive Asatru (Norse Religion), I think a number of people would be interested as well.

***

"When does the crazy stop?"

When each one of us, this moment, stops *doing* the crazy, *doing* the misery, *doing* the fear and division, *doing* the mask of personality and doing all *doing* that was adopted, not by our intention, but imposed outside by others who put all of these habits like a straightjacket over our innocent intelligence starting from birth onwards.

There are no masses of people to make sane. The energy of identification people put in belonging to them spreads what little self-awareness they have into a mob mentality that suppresses the only "unit" that has the power and potential understanding to stop the "crazy."

It is you, the individual.

Without you understanding, there can be no drop of doing the crazy on its own accord.

Only you can become aware of the "stop." There is no one else on Earth to be concerned about whether they can stop or not.

You are the world itself.

And there is great potential if you understand this, with your whole mass coming alive, then the craziness in your life begins to drop away. You become a light unto your Self and live, think, love and celebrate your life as an example.

Don't make it a missionary thing. Just live your life among the others and let them in their freedom recognize it or not. Be drawn to you or not.

My briefest answer to your friend to her question is just one word:

Meditation...

Meditation is the "Noah's Ark of Consciousness." The only Ark available to us in the Great Flood of madness overtaking a world that has too many billions of people polluting the psycho-sphere as well as the ecosphere. We are polluting the atmosphere and it is upsetting the ecological balance of the planet. The psychic dimension of our spirit atmosphere is also being polluted by an overload of thoughts, the mind and emotional noise, so to speak.

The native peoples of the world made me aware of this problem in the late 1980s. That the world is under the influence of a *Mind Plague* and as the population will soon complete adding another billion—making it eight billion people on this planet—the mob minded, herd madness of the human lemming effect will intensify all around the world.

That's my short answer. What follows is the long and comprehensive answer: this book, this Rebel's Manifesto.

I invite you all to share my personal as well as prophetic journey, and understand how I came to tell you the above short answer.

CHAPTER ONE
Noah's Ark of Consciousness

The Prophecy and a Messenger

Man is now living in his most critical moment and it is a crisis of immense dimensions. Either he will die or a new man will be reborn...It is going to be a death and resurrection. Unless human consciousness changes totally man cannot survive. As he is right now he is already outdated.

...During this period there will be every kind of destruction on Earth including natural catastrophes and man manufactured auto-suicidal efforts. In other words there will be floods which have never been known since the time of Noah, along with earthquakes, volcanic eruptions and everything else that is possible through nature.

The Earth cannot tolerate this type of mankind any longer. There will be wars which are bound to end in nuclear explosions, hence no ordinary Noah's ark is going to save humanity. ...The Holocaust is not going to be confined to certain places, it is going to be global so no escape will be possible. You can only escape within and that's what I teach. I do not teach worship of God or any other ritual but only a scientific way of coming to your innermost core. (Osho [1983])

The mother of all travails is unavoidable. There will be famines, plagues, and global disasters, whether seers have used the gift of true providence to forewarn us of signs of the end times, or have conditioned us to make the end times happen. A tribulation is coming, whether it is the end of the world or the birth pangs of a new age. The year 2012 will come and soon be forgotten as we advance deeper into a century of revolution and upheaval. The 2010s will pass into the *Roaring 2020s* that will see unprecedented stress brought to bear on human civilization and Earth's ecology. There will be wars, global warming and unrest. By the 2020s there will be billions of young people expecting a better future, but their own excessive numbers will disenfranchise them. They will see the job market and the world's resources collapse. The basics for happiness in life will be denied them. They will not enjoy a good education, or a roof over their head. They will be denied food, water and hope. The young will be prime targets for the harangues and hate mongering of not one but dozens of messianic Hitlers preaching an apocalyptic solution.

If only they could catch a ride on a Rapture cloud—if there were one. The more practical person might dig a survivalist's ditch and wait out the tribulation to come, but escape may not be possible when the whole world is going to feel the pain of this multifaceted travail. If food runs out during a protracted global famine, the survivalists will be the first doomsday moles rooted out of their holes by the desperate who are digging up the last of the hoarded supplies.

No one will escape.

You may choose to abandon the rising, flooding coastlines of California for a religiously pure and safe area like the desert town of Sedona, Arizona; but rather than drown from rising oceans, you may desiccate when the potable water in that New Age Mecca runs out.

The coming decades of the early twenty-first century could see all of us writhing under an Internet of history's first global emergency. No region, no nation and no person on Earth will be exempt from the effects of another person's misuse or overuse of the planet. The next 30 years will endure floods not seen in recorded history—if not directly from weather, then from rising coastlines.

Prophets foresee earthquakes, volcanic eruptions, and even many scientists predict natural disasters of a scope and magnitude never before encountered. Earth appears to be rebelling against a humanity that chooses to remain retarded while it waits for the saviors to fix them.

Nostradamus and other seers have predicted a plague of 70 wars across the world, triggered by the breakdown of water and food resources caused by rampant overpopulation. A few of these wars will end in nuclear explosions and the unleashing of biological and chemical-weapon plagues.

Attempts to escape may not only be futile but also result in a missed opportunity. A major theme promoted by more renegade redeemers—those mystics who do not tow the mainstream anti-life and pro-afterlife line of the Second Coming Syndrome—is that you cannot escape from yourself. No matter how high the Rapture carries you into the clouds, no matter how many Himalayan mountains you pull over your head to escape the disasters in your survivalist hole, the problem comes along for the ride.

You are the problem.

And you could be the answer.

The answer to averting the tribulations to come may arise out of each individual understanding and transcending the problem he or she has become.

Individual salvation requires something else entirely, a totally new vector. Though some continue to wait for rescue by an Ark or a New Jerusalem to mother-ship them out of harm's way, there are visions that act like irritating flies dancing on the nose of such deliverance dreams, disturbing their reverie. These visions buzz with images of a travail from which there's no escape. They say that the coming disasters will force all people to stand face to face with a heartbreaking and dream-breaking reality: No saints or saviors are coming to save us from ourselves.

We will have to become our own saviors.

One of the renegade mystics, Osho, believes the next Noah's ark needed to save humanity is a *Noah's Ark of Consciousness*. It is not a UFO mothership of nebulous construction built for one to wait out the seven years of tribulation behind a comet's tail. It isn't a cave city for survivalists. It is a hideaway so secret that you'd never guess how close it nudges against where you live even at this moment. It hides right behind the source of your existence.

This safe haven is a place that spiritual survivalists retreat to.

It is the Ark of Consciousness within each of us.

The pathway to this ark can be found by remaining silent and centered exactly in the middle of the cyclone of the coming times.

Meditation: Therapy for Madhouse Earth

While watching the changing world outside and the movement of thoughts and emotions within, I become more aware of a presence that doesn't change. It is impossible to define in words what this is, but I do know that it is always the same presence; that when it comes, it is everywhere and nowhere at once; that nothing I'm thinking or feeling can connect with it; that it is so still it doesn't exist and so subtle that at times it is too alive to bear.

I remember first encountering this presence as a child. Then I lost touch with it. The losing was a gradual process called growing up. I experienced it as walling up. Gradually Pink Floyd's bricks piled up around me, blocking out the limitless view of the innocent and unnamable wonder that a child feels by just being alive. I was taught to hold on to thoughts and possess emotional expectations; in short, I was given recipes for accepted adult behavior. I painfully learned to live in a world where beauty and the art of being alive are pushed lower and lower on life's laundry list; I was taught to survive in a culture where cars, money, face-saving at all costs, and manipulation of others are the primary values. I had come into the world as a cosmos and it looked like I would leave the world as a spent commodity.

When it got to be too much, I was pushed to the edge of a nervous breakthrough. There were only two alternatives: rediscover what I had lost, or lose myself.

How can I tell you about this journey inward to find my self again, without tarnishing it with judgments, dialectics, words?

If I ever greet you beyond the veil of these words, we might find a way to share this mystery called *meditation*. I will not speak of it, I will sing it to you, dance it; we will hug meditation, we will *silent* meditation. Our sutras will be giggles. I'd rather not use words, but this is the Kali Yuga after all—an age that uses the least adequate media to express the deepest truths.

With that said, let's stumble ahead in the darkness of print:

I do not yet know *who* I am but meditation allows me to often see *how* I am.

Through understanding the hows of my happiness-sadness-love-and-hate, I observe their rough-and-tumble within me with greater distance. Meditation helps me to watch the movement of my thoughts and emotions. I become more a spectator than a participant in stress, pain, and denial. Through meditation I have been able to uncover the root cause of all my misery: The fear of change, and lurking behind that, the ultimate fear—the fear of death. Meditation has helped me observe the mechanics of misery and fear.

There's a Sufi metaphor about identification. Misery doesn't come to us, we unconsciously seek it out and hold on to it, like flinging our arms around a pillar. As we squeeze tighter we yell, "Oh, if I only could be rid of this misery and pain!"

This misunderstanding is our choice. As American mystic Adi Da Samraj once remarked, we *do* misery, we *do* expectation.

Hell is not a place. We *do* it.

We *do* predictability.

We make prophecy work because we are so damned predictable. Caught in the cycles of time and unconsciousness, we have repeated again and again the behaviors that make it easy for the seers to prophesy us unto doomsday.

The crossroads in time where we find ourselves now demands a spiritual rebellion that can prevent us from doing an apocalypse of doom in all dimensions. The first decades of this new century require that a significant number of people get some distance from themselves to see how they tick. Then the original meaning of Apocalypse can be remembered. They can "lift the veil" of illusion. Doomsday can become the *Bloom-Day* of the Mystic Rose.

There is a need for a global awareness of how, from the moment we emerge from the womb, we are programmed from birth onwards to imprint concepts that are totally divorced from our deepest natural understanding of life. Only when there are enough people ready to rebel against this ancient circle of programmed misery and predictability can it be broken.

The spiritual rebels will certainly be in the minority. Most of us are bound to avoid encountering the raw revelation that we actually love our misery and hold its pillar fast to our breasts while we wish and wail for a new age. In the coming decade, billions will discover that misery and fear is all they know. But unlike most people, the spiritual rebels will break out of their prison of conditioning and become the new humanity arising out of the rubble of the old.

The spiritual rebels will not pander to the death cults of current religious thought; they will live *this* life so fully that heaven will exist inside them, not somewhere in the afterworld. They will escape from their jail-keeper called God. And they will slip from the bonds of national identification to become citizens of the world.

Meditation is the method to uncover all the illusions that keep humanity in bondage. It is the only hope this planet has to avoid the collision course so many seers down the centuries have predicted for us. Every misunderstanding and distortion of truth that has blindly dragged us to the brink of the precipice will have to be jettisoned, if we are not to plunge over the edge at the end of the 2020s.

This is why the emergence of the new breed, *Homo novus*—the true strangers among us, is viewed with suspicion and fear. The priests or the politicians cannot control these people. They do not pray for happiness, they *are* happiness. In the midst of a suicidal world, their way of life exposes the death wish society must encounter and transcend if it is to survive.

The spiritual rebels are the soul and spirit of the new Golden Age. And meditation is their new science.

My own journey into meditation and spiritual rebellion began from a nasty experience I had as a seven year old, when I moved to a new school in a new neighborhood.

I was in love with the little girl sitting next to me in my second-grade class. When she was moved to another spot in the classroom, I was brokenhearted. The teacher, like many adults I knew then (and now), liked to hide her fears behind a façade of power. She looked as big as her fear, and when she demanded to know what was the matter with me, I didn't speak in words but in pain, and sobbed into my hands. My expression of naked feeling elicited from kids and teacher alike an immediate wave of hostility and derision. For weeks after that event, I was treated with disgust and fear, rejected as some kind of *thing*.

During an atomic air raid drill for World War III—so common in the years following the Cuban Missile Crisis—I accidentally bumped into the largest kid in the class while groping in the dark classroom for my place to *duck and cover* myself.

His immediate reaction was to slug me in the stomach.

Crying, doubled over in agony, I asked him why he hit me. Still a kid and not yet completely formed into the proper masked and label-loving adult, he was struck by the blow of my existential question.

"I don't know!" he blinked, bewildered. "It's what dad told me to do. When you're hit, hit back."

That was my first hard lesson in programming.

It got worse. When he and a gang of kids would chase me off the playground every recess with tetherballs and stones, I had to run my little ass into a nearby storm drain trench. As I huddled there, I was forced to face the reality that people were neither sane nor loving; they only pretended to be. The children would forget about me and wander back to the swings and sandboxes, but I could never forget this heartbreaking truth, heartbreaking because it set me apart from people. It made me aware that I am alone.

But no bitter experience is without its sweetness. Crouching in the trench, chin buried in the pungent grass, with tearful, wide eyes gazing at dancing clouds in a silent sky, I also became aware that Nature did not—could not—reject me. It was more than a friend, it was a beloved. As I became aware of my aloneness, Nature accepted it. *Was* it.

After that I could not see fear in Nature, only innocence. There is no judgment in Nature's stases and catastrophes. It is unnatural man, divided against the Self, who judges them. There is life, death, violence and peace flowing from animals, earth and plants. They don't judge or feel divisions like we do. The rosebush doesn't compare itself to the lotus and commit suicide. In fact, no animal except man commits suicide or indiscriminately slaughters its own kind. We compare, and throw our minds and hearts into the turmoil of division. This division becomes projected onto all of our relationships with other human beings and with the Earth. As we become more and more split off from our fellow humans and from the planet, we create all the conditions that draw us closer to death—personal and global.

The insights of my personal apocalypse made it hard for me to buy into all the ways people suppress the natural within and destroy the ecology of Earth with their fearful greed. A new and tender consciousness arose that at the time had no words. Looking back on it years later, I realized it was then I made the commitment that has forever sabotaged my efforts to embrace life as it is socially presented and commonly accepted. That is why I walked away from a promising career as an opera singer. I didn't fit with anyone's projections and expectations.

I somehow understood in my child-mind that a truly natural, spiritual person would be as silent as that sky, as playful as those eddying clouds, as rich with the fragrance of wisdom as the grass cushioning my chin. A natural human being, like the grass, could not dictate or push his or her fragrance on others but would simply be unable to contain it.

In the intensity of that terrible moment of rejection, Nature showed me how to sniff out an authentic member of the genus *Homo novus*. These flowers in humanity's manure field would possess the silence of Nature and an equanimity in the face of Nature's two polar complementaries—destruction and creation. I would instinctively recognize these members of the new human race by their laughter and celebration uncaused, by the gleam of a second and consciously recognized childhood sparking in their eyes. I would know them if their silent gaze and presence were not disturbed by fame or infamy, riches or poverty, life or death. They would remain inwardly blissful, unaffected by life's vagaries or any attempts by those outside of their silence to abuse and disturb them. The *Homo novus* would be happy in a palace or in the dirtiest holding cell. And if sadness on rare occasions came to their doors, they would watch it rather than indulge it, until sadness moved on.

I have spent the last thirty-seven years traveling around the world in search of such men and women. I have found them. They are my critera for saying you and I are unnatural. They have also showed me—in their unique ways—that meditation, the science of self-observation, is the only medicine that can cure the insanity we have become and give us back a future.

I do not ask or expect you to believe me. In fact, there is no point in either believing or debunking what I'm saying without a sincere and intimate investigation on your own.

I am satisfied with the ongoing process of my own apocalypse. I have met a few members of the genus *Homo novus* and their fragrance is meditation.

The words *meditation* and *medicine* have the same ancient root. One heals the body, the other the soul. If we look from a more occidental angle, the words *meditation* and *mechanic* also have the same roots. If you can watch your entire mental-emotional engine without getting caught in its grinding gears, if you can see it as the dispassionate and watchful *mechanic*, you will then find ways to fix your *engine*. It will start working for you rather than disturb your ride through life.

I can thank the apocalypse of meditation for pushing me out of an operatic career. Nine months before I had my *nervous breakthrough*, I became interested in meditation as a way to relieve stress and refresh my body-mind. But I soon found out that meditation was more than a mere exercise in positive thinking or an exercise in creative visualizations to find new and improved love and abundant money and health. Taking twenty minutes a day to watch my breath turned my outward focus in. This turning *in* did more than slow the heartbeat and ward off high blood pressure of the upwardly mobile professional I had become. It reminded me of childhood's timeless time when trees fall and nobody is there to hear, when flowers grow with nobody there to see, and feelings flow with nobody there to feel.

Through watching the simple witnessing of life's infinite movements I unearthed the pleasure in paradox.

I rediscovered moments when life became poetry again.

When roots of silence sink where I sit so still soaking earth softly. And deep silence dives in skies caught cavorting behind closed eyes.

Meditation started washing my *looking* with eternity's twinkle.

After a few months of practicing simple Zen exercises of watching the breath, I couldn't understand why something so pleasurable and revitalizing wasn't universally practiced. Then a moment came when the new awareness reached deeper into my unconscious and threw a shattering light on my illusions.

It can happen at any moment. Especially if you watch your breath, if you are still, waiting. Something trips the existential switch and the screen of your personal id soap operas blinks out. A void fills the void, wiggling through a brief crack in the noise of the mind. It is the apocalypse of truth breaking the sliding bolt that locks away all the lies from one's sight. It is a thief in the night, stealth-like and silent, a wave, invisible, undermining one's cliff of solid ego.

In one unguarded moment I became transparent. And though the *guard* of moments—the personality—instantly returned, I could not completely forget the void's abiding and spacious sky of silence.

For me, this was and is the threshold of meditation. It is as much a death as a delight. Meditation's techniques of self-observation showed me my thoughts were no more mine to possess than a wind racing through empty dreams.

At meditation's first penetration, I became aware that this "John Hogue" was a fiction written by many hands—none of them my own. A name, a religion, a country, and finally a personality had been applied like bricks, imprisoning the authentic being my mother and father had brought into the world.

Early on, the label bricks were of soft and pliable mud, easy for a child to break free of, but between the ages of seven and fourteen, the bricks turned into unyielding stone. I had become my own memorial statue while still living.

The child seized these brick labels as greedily as he seized the tit. What else could he do? That child needed the grown-ups, and the grown-ups felt they needed to condition him for the coming life of lies and limitations. The child of silence became a gullible youth who listened to society's learned hypocrites—the priests of impossible horizons—who, save for the noise of their roaring, have never encountered the things they taught: gods, heavens, and hells.

The youth became imprisoned in adulthood's emotional and psychic castle. At the age of twenty-one, meditation's taste of disidentification made John aware that his *buddha* had atrophied. The Enlightened One reduced to *enlightened once.* Fear had become his bedmate, denial, the sheets.

Like medicines, meditation can be bitter. Initially, it can give you worse pain than the disease itself. Cancer patients would like to escape the only therapies that might possibly save them, but if they choose to fight for life, painful chemotherapy or radiation will be risked.

After abandoning an operatic career, I began taking risks. I again started asking all those questions children ask and adults avoid. Essential questions: Why am I unhappy? Why do I fear? Who am I?

At first I tried the usual New Age assortment of meditations that heightened psychic powers. After four years of this, I could see auras, read minds, etc. Still, the essential facticity of my being was hidden. While astral traveling I had many fascinating experiences, but they didn't make me any more aware of *who* was zipping in and out of the astral realms. Who was seeing auras? Who indeed was opening his chakras? Who was reading minds? Who was this mystery that sometimes accurately saw the future?

Whether I am looking at a cup of coffee or seeing my past and future lives, how can any of these experiences be me?

Who, after all, is *the watcher*?

Frustration led me away from the psychic seeker-sucking game to an exploration of many Eastern techniques of classical meditation such as Yoga and Vipassana—which is Buddha's technique of sitting watching the *suchness* of thoughts and emotions. I also had direct experiences with some new and radical seeds of Eastern meditation set to sprout in the West sometime in the early twenty first century.

Since I began my inner quest in the late 1970s, I have encountered what in my opinion were many charlatans and also a handful of authentic masters. An account of these spiritual examinations, meditation therapies and teachers would be too vast to describe here. A detailed account will be forthcoming in future books.

Here, I can only touch on some of the radically new ideas about meditation that have been introduced in the latter half of the twentieth century. For instance, if you fly to the town of Pune (Poona), India, just 100 kilometers from the labyrinth city of Mumbai (Bombay), you will encounter the most striking examples of this. Nestled in the town that gave Tantra one of its greatest ancient centers, the birthplace of one of India's most significant twentieth-century mystics, Meher Baba, is the Ashram (spiritual campus) that used to be known as Osho Commune International in the late 1980s and after the beginning of the new century is best known around the world as the Osho International Meditation Resort.

There you will find the disciples of the late Osho carrying on their master's vision of providing a Club Meditation for the creation of the new humanity. It is a sixty-eight-acre resort of luscious gardens, black granite and marble buildings and pyramids, a strange contrast to the surrounding squalor of a bustling Third World city.

It has undergone many alterations since I first entered its gates back in 1980, when it was known as the Poona Ashram of the notorious sex guru Bhagwan Shree Rajneesh. I had gone there two years prior to my longer stay at the Rajneeshee Ranch in Oregon. While the later experiment allowed me the opportunity to sample social experiments in future living, the Poona Ashram offered me a taste of life at the frontiers of the Human Potential Movement.

In *Nostradamus and the Millennium* (1987), the first volume of my Nostradamus prophecy trilogy (the second and third volumes are *Nostradamus, The New Revelations* [1994] and *Nostradamus: The Complete Prophecies* [1997]), I examined predictions of Nostradamus regarding the loose fellowship of therapists and meditation movements of the last fifty years known as the Human Potential Movement. Nostradamus pegged this movement as the source of tomorrow's spiritual rebellion. I was determined to find out what it was all about.

Frankly, when I did, it shocked me. Up until I became acquainted with these new therapy movements, I never knew that screaming, pillow beating, or openly exploring my sexuality in a therapy group could be the beginning of treading an authentic spiritual path. When I first heard about the ashram, I was told they practiced the most cathartic meditation technique in the movement. At first it was called Chaotic Meditation; then the name was changed to Dynamic Meditation. I was about to find out what it was, firsthand.

Osho is famous in meditation circles for his controversial claim that we moderns, particularly the Westernized variety, are the most restless and neurotic humans who have ever existed. With enough forceful discipline, we may be able to keep our body still, but we cannot still our minds. Vipassana, Yoga, and all the rest of the 112 techniques from the East are made for simpler people of more innocent and less complex times.

Before sitting in silence can happen, the accumulation of stress, anger, and repression packed away behind modern people's happy-face masks has to be creatively and safely expressed. Osho claimed to have a meditation technique that, if practiced all over the world every morning, could be used as a release valve for all the pent-up collective angers that periodically erupt in a binge of global slaughter—what I've coined as the *will to catharsis*.

The meditation has five sections and is done to especially composed music by the New Age composer Deuter as conceived by Osho. During the first part, of ten minutes duration, you breathe rapidly, chaotically and deeply through the nose. This is supposed to build up the energy that can help you release the flame of pent-up repressions.

Then, at the sound of a gong, the music changes into waves of sonic wildness. For the second ten minutes you are to undergo catharsis, release emotions, anger, laughter, tears, gibberish, fear, rage, madness—whatever comes up. You are to dance it, shake it, scream it, sing it, but you are absolutely not allowed to hurt others in the hall.

The third gong brings on a ten-minute hop of heaven-hell. You stop releasing emotions [or stop undergoing catharsis] and reach your arms straight over your head and jump to the pulsing synthesizers and drums. Every time your feet hit the ground you yell *Hoo!* with all you've got, as if it meant life or death. This is a variation of a Sufi technique designed to bring your energies up out of your sex center and take them through the rest of your body.

At the last hop and *Hoo!* the pre-recorded voice of Osho yelling *Stop!* cuts the music like splitting a thunderbolt. You then freeze in place like a statue for fifteen minutes and watch within.

Finally, there is fifteen minutes of dancing and celebrating.

The first three sections are consciously constructed to completely exhaust you. In this way, Osho's techniques are similar to those of George Gurdjieff and the meditation schools of central Asia who believe that man had deeper and deeper layers of energy—second winds, if you will—that first have to be expended before real meditation can happen. The more total your exhaustion, the deeper the plunge within your being.

Many mystics, past and present, say that only when one reaches a crisis can an authentic spiritual journey begin. A state of extreme urgency is a must. Totality is the ultimate credential. Only when the inner search becomes a life-and-death issue can the tension be brought to the breaking point and send you into an altered state of deep relaxation.

Dynamic Meditation uses the first three sections to prepare you for the state of dispassionate witnessing that is the final preparation for meditation. The rapid breathing brings up the repressed tensions; the catharsis stage then activates a good spiritual vomit; the hopping nearly exhausts you, bringing the body to the limit of its endurance, and then you can fall into an altered state—a meditator's version of a runner's high, so to speak.

My understanding of meditation techniques is that they relax you into witnessing. These techniques themselves, however, are not true meditation, nor are all those so-called spiritual experiences one has through being still and silent. Meditation is not an experience. Meditation is not a thing one does to get something, but it does seem that some preparation for meditation is needed. The silent witnessing of meditation only blossoms from the waiting, the allowing, the parking of the body-mind, the deep relaxation without a goal or expectations, because to have goals and expectations is to be tense.

Back in 1980 in India when Dynamic Meditation was first described to me, it was enough to stir a volcano of rage and fear underneath my spiritual façade. The night before doing my first Dynamic Mediation was one of the darkest in my life. I experienced the essence behind the terrible words of St. John's prophecy about people trying to pull the mountains over themselves to escape facing the revelation of truth. That night moments passed like the peeling of skin. I tossed and turned, then ran to the bathroom and saw the puffy face and slit eyes of a man stunned by his own terror.

I never felt so stuck. I could not go back and I did not want to go forward into the unknown that a cathartic meditation would reveal. I writhed about in the damp fishing net of my bed covers in a tropical-fever night, cursing myself, Osho, meditation, and all the mystics that disturb people's sleep.

I could sense that if I went too far with this meditation experiment I would reach a point when I could no longer return to that deep sleep. I tell you, reader: since my experience of that night I see a terrible revelation about everyone—we don't want to wake up. We don't want happiness, we don't want *real* freedom because to attain it we must confront all that is false in us, chaining us down. To be a meditator is to be mother to the birth of our own inner child. The master or the meditation technique is the midwife. They can help, they can hold your hand, they can indicate what you have to do, but the pain of giving birth to yourself is encountered alone. No one else feels the contractions of your womb like you do.

When the time came, I somehow managed to drag myself like a condemned criminal to the ashram in time to be under the wide, wall-less tent dome of the meditation hall before Dynamic began at 6:00 am. sharp. There I mingled with several hundred groggy meditators. We blew our noses and blindfolded ourselves, digging bare feet into the cold cement floor. All braced themselves for the first gong, which would strip the predawn air of its silence with Deuter's apocalyptic muzak.

At the sound of the gong, the knotted rubber band of my pent-up terrors released its prop and off went my model-plane personality into the predawn darkness.

By the end of the third stage of Dynamic, if I had any ambition for nirvana left, the hopping and *hooing* was squeezing it to the relaxing point. When the recorded blast of *STOP!* cut the sweaty air, I froze-fell to the cold floor. For fifteen minutes, I became a stillness floating on the waves of a gasping-for-breath—too tired to think, too cleaned by catharsis to be afraid.

What can I say to you about this heap of John Hogue lying on the cement floor? What words can convey the down-down-

down, deeper-deeper-deeper he had become for those eternal minutes?

Clear, because nothing obstructs.
Soundless, because it has no end of depth.
No bottom for the sounding,
No surface for the sounder.
IT—looking without eyes and dying
without death.

A cloud of darkness, I gave my self in rains,
Letting fall showers of sorrow,
Until a burning sky of joy remains.

The delicate notes of the flute heralding the final stage of Dynamic Meditation brought the first awareness of that inner sky to me. Drained limbs made an effort to move, twitching like a fresh corpse. The music caressed more movements out of my still pool of exhaustion until I was able to lift my heavy, blindfolded head. At that moment, I was drowned in an explosion of brilliant white light as bracing as a cold mountain stream. The light took me up in its embrace. Where one exhausted man lay a moment before, there appeared a dancing fool.

In my veins fired life, dyeing the darkness in countless fire clouds. To dance was to touch gold with eyes and bathe the world with sight. By the end of the celebration music, and as the rising sun cut shafts of light through birdcalls and the tropical plants surrounding the hall, I had become the blue-viewing of sky.

Now when the world's misery pours tears out of my eyes, they are not only of suffering or the grieving spawn of expectations and desires, they are the realization that sanity is possible. Humans suffer because they cannot completely return to an animal's innocent state. I am one human who is convinced that all humans suffer life on Earth because to one degree or another they have sand chaffing their dreams. They hurt because they have the destiny—mostly ignored and repressed—to make within themselves a pearl called *Homo novus*, the New Humanity.

Prophecy indicates that time is running out for the birth of this new humanity. The birth has to happen this very moment through a spiritual rebellion against the past. Humankind is destined for a catharsis, a psychic breakdown that can also become a psychic breakthrough. The choice is ours.

The Coming Mind Broil

Many native prophetic traditions the world over share a version of the world's physical and psychic energy fields rising a third or more in intensity in the coming century. They contend that the earth's energy band began its increase between 1983 and 1991, and will attain to its higher vibration around 2012. It is said that this new frequency of energy will be a blessing to those who can embrace the unknown, and who are open to innovation, adventure, and meditation. However, the native seers and shamans warn that those who hold on to fear and contraction will find life after 2012 hard to endure. Some will enjoy mind-liberation, while those who cannot change will suffer a mind-broil. Those individuals who cannot abandon fossilized ideas and traditions will be so subconsciously terrified by the new energies of new times that it is said they will drop dead from their own fear.

Tribal people will tell you that thoughts are things, and that modern humankind uses the subtle forces of thought most irresponsibly When there were relatively few of us, this didn't have a serious impact, but now the unprecedented appearance of unaware and mechanically conditioned humans contributes more aberrant and unconscious thoughts than ever before.

When the critical mass of so many unconscious thoughts may cause a foretold psychic trauma, only the ark of a silent mind may keep its cool in the brainstorms to come.

Shit Happens to Sleepwalkers

One night a man opens his eyes, rolls out of bed, and starts walking to the kitchen. He passes his wife coming out of the bathroom on her way back to bed, says good morning—then bellies up to the kitchen counter and relieves himself in the trash can under the kitchen sink.

That's when he wakes up.

I was once a witness to an experiment in autosuggested somnambulism at an after-high-school party. A young woman agreed to go under hypnosis. The hypnotizer suggested that she had now gone home and it was time to take a shower. Before my disbelieving eyes, the woman began to disrobe in front of us. She did so with complete innocence. It wasn't an act. She was alone behind the door in the bathroom of her mind. The 15 equally embarrassed and amazed onlookers did not exist to her. We stopped the experiment, and the hypnotizer asked her to button up her blouse before she exposed herself further. Once awakened from the trance, she had no memory of what she had done and thought we were all joking.

People function remarkably well while they are sleepwalking. They can assume the illusion of full cognizance, especially when under the spell of someone else's hypnotic suggestions.

With that in mind, relax, please relax...r-e-l-a-x...let your eyes follow the pendulum of my words back and forth...back and forth... Allow your mind to open, slowly...s-l-o-w-ly...as I suggest to you the following bedtime story:

Once upon a time, in another life, I was born into a world where everyone I knew, from the first moment of life onward, conspired to put me back to sleep. I lived in a land where parents, pedagogues, and priests taught me that slumber was wakefulness. I was a good pupil, because I had no understanding of the difference between being awake and dreaming of being awake. The more seemingly awake I became, the more the spell of dreaming deepened.

In that life they taught me to make every waking aim and effort a means to catch hold of noble illusions such as success, happiness in love, fulfillment in children, contentment in possessions—and last but not least, they taught me to dream of being mortal, virtuous, and worthy of God's salvation.

They taught me to see things upside down from what they were. For instance, the priest waved his smoking censer back and forth, back and forth, in blessing…b-l-e-s-s-i-n-g…telling me repeatedly that Christ was my savior, Christ was my savior, believe… b-e-l-i-e-v-e… believe only in Him. Shut out all the suggestions of other religions and you will be saved.

As I was growing up, each of my parents taught me the difference between right and wrong, waving a mesmerizing finger from side to side. The teacher instructed, waving her chalk stick back and forth before my eyes before putting it into my hand to chalk out her somnambulistic mantras for being a dutiful matriculate.

I began to fill my empty ledger of a soul with hypnotizing dictums, such as to honor and obey without question ideas and traditions you never had a hand (or a say) in creating— especially if they uphold traditions your hypnagogic demagogues never questioned yet held in dumbfounded respect. I was especially spellbound by the Word of God and the promised return of the Messiah. In Sunday school I fumbled for my Bible and they helped me relax…relax…and count back from Psalms 150 to 1. They counted me back through all the verses of all the holy books until my "I" was Mesmer-I-zed to automatically do good deeds—not for the simple joy of just doing them, mind you, but to gain something in return, to earn a place in the last and best dream: heaven.

If I was to get by in a society of somnambulism it was necessary to have my priests and teachers gas me up to dream the world in black and white. They therefore implanted many delayed reactions to anything that would compromise the dream. The priests and therapists helped me make contracts on love. I played Ken in phenol-Barbie-doll dreams about love and marriage.

Above all, they programmed me to expect. Expect... e-x-p-e-c-t... deeper... and... deeper... beyond the intelligence that doubts...beyond the heart that senses...to sink deeper beyond the kith and kinesthesia of the body's natural instincts...to fall into the cruise control of expectation. Expect others to love you...to fulfill you. And if they don't, then always...a-l-w-a-y-s...blame the other.

Naturally good dreams have a way of snuggling next to nightmares. That fact wasn't overlooked by my Svengali social programmers. If my worldly dreams remained unfulfilled, that too was kept under control by deeply implanted suggestions, like "getting religious."

Renounce Barbie as plastic! Renounce the catalepsy of this world. Dream a higher dream. Be narcotized by the glory of God. Go beyond this physical dream body. "Phantomize" about the paradise promised to you in the other world. Reject the dream of the hedonist and sinner for the dream of the renouncer and the saint. Having once been completely engrossed by greed for money, I now rolled over in my slumber to obsess over cultivating my love of God.

There was nothing I couldn't do in the land of Nod, as long as I didn't wake up. Above all, I was not to doubt the dream. I was even free to visualize anarchy and rebellion as long as I stayed within the dreamscape. Revolutions are welcomed in the world-dream as long as they sustain an illusion of progress, as long as they only decorate the tight lips of established power with a new lipstick. Revolutions are rubbed into the stiff upper lip of power periodically to change the pigment of history's fancy. Yesterday it was communism red, today it is capitalist red, white, and blue.

To protect me from the apocalypse of awakening from my sleep, my religious and social educators painted bitter salve on the hangnails of my doubts to sour the impulse to bite and chew on them.

I somnolently lived out my life in the land of Nod, one more citizen of the nation of "as if," worshiping the God of "around-and-about the truth." And before my death woke me up, I dreamed of waking up in heaven.

Come back...come b-a-c-k.... On the count of one...two...three millenniums of sleepwalking through history.
One...two...three...
Snap out of it!
Come back to full consciousness.

Wha...what's this?! Am I pissing in the kitchen trash can? Am I mechanically exposing myself in front of leering voyeurs beyond the walls of my make-believe shower stall? Somebody's put me under the trance of three hundred religions. Their hypnotic suggestion has me thinking we're all alone and fine in our bathrooms, stripping off our sins and earning points for heaven when we might instead be peeling off our awareness and intelligence, exposing ourselves to trouble
One...two...three...at the count of 2020.
Return me to humanity before it is too late. Or else I may never wake up from an overdose of doomsday suggestion pills.

Many rebel mystics tell us that for most of human history people have lived a somnambulistic life. For such people, history is just something that happens. They are so much leafy debris cast helplessly into the fateful flailing-about of history's whirlwinds. The winds blow them *hither* into the storm clouds of their wars and dark ages, and *yawn* into still quiet heaps of momentary idleness in times of peace. Their eyes are as opened as those of the blind who reason that Providence has led them one day to stumble into a bed of flowers rather than a tiger trap.

The consequence of unconsciousness may not be a punishment by God-somebody, but a self-created breakdown of individuals and systems. End time may be a hypnotic suggestion fulfilled by potentially conscious beings if they live life in a sleepy and robotic way. They pop the sleeping pill—perchance to dream that their planet can endlessly tolerate their abuse. And if it can't sustain civilization in the twenty-first century, then they inhale a whole bottle of tranquilizing prophetic promises that a messiah will save them.

Safe Is the Center of the Cyclone
Outside, the freezing desert night.
This other night inside grows warm, kindling.
Let the landscape be covered with thorny crust.
We have a soft garden in here.
The continents blasted,
cities and little towns, everything
become a scorched blackened ball.
The news we hear is full of grief for the future,
but the real news inside here
Is there's no news at all

Mevlana Jalaluddin Rumi (1207-1273) In the Poem "The Tent"
Translated by Coleman Barks from *The Essential Rumi* (1995)

When Mevlana Rumi was 12, his father, Bahauddin Veled, a noted Islamic scholar and teacher, led his family out of Balkh (Afghanistan) as refugees from the thundering hooves of the Mongol hordes of Genghis Khan. Starting in 1219, the savage Mongolian horsemen descended on the Persian Empire from the Central Asian steppes. Wherever the Mongols rampaged, whole cities were burned to the ground and their entire population of men, women, and children were slaughtered.

The boy who would become one of Sufism's greatest enlightened mystics and poets spent a number of his formative years enduring many nights under the elements and days of hardship, uncertainty, and hunger as he wandered westward with his family across the devastated lands and burned-out cities of the Persian Empire. Veled and his family finally settled in the relative safety of Konya, Turkey, where Rumi could eventually grow to manhood and succeed his father as the head of the local medrese (Dervish-leaning community).

Konya was the cosmopolitan gateway to the famous Silk Road. In those days, the city lived in a state of constant religious agitation. When political intrigue and religious pontificating failed, different religious communities often settled disputes with clubs and knives over whose creed or prophet was better. Strangely enough, all the warring factions accepted Rumi, in part because of his loving inclusiveness and acceptance for all.

It is said that he had an aura of silence and calmness that was unflappable and infectious. He composed the poem (above) sometime in the 1250s, when terrified traders riding down the Silk Road to Konya from the East exacerbated the civic strife with tales of a new wave of apocalyptic devastation coming from the descendants of Genghis Khan. The Mongol horse armies of his grandsons would unleash their own version of Operation Desert Storm, obliterating Islam's glorious Abbasid capital of Baghdad.

When the news reached Rumi and his disciples that Mongols were riding up and down the plains and deserts of the Near East with impunity, there was indeed reason to fear and grieve for the future. Yet his recorded observations on the matter testify to how little impact the negative effect of childhood traumas had on his inner peace.

Rumi the man, like Rumi the former child refugee, viewed the outside world from the silent haven of his inner "ark" of consciousness.

Where Christ suffers famously on his cross and complains to his father-God in heaven about it, al-Hillaj Mansoor—a little-known 10th-century Islamic mystic—faces without complaint a crucifixion many times more barbaric and cruel. He presses prayerful hands to God one last time before the headsmen chop them off. He thanks the butchered feet piled before his leg stumps for taking him on his journeys of self-discovery. He gives his crying disciples, the jeering mob, and his murderers equal regard. He looks upon them with happy and loving eyes until the moment those eyes are gouged out of their sockets. After this al-Hillaj turns his head to heaven. The head no longer has a nose, or ears—the executioner has already sliced them off. But al-Hillaj still has a rapturous smile. He gazes heavenward without eyes, spreading his arm-stumps as if they still possess open, beseeching hands in praise of Allah.

Al-Hillaj sings the following verse: "Love of the One is isolation of the One. Those that believe not therein seek to hasten it: but those who believe in it go in fear of it, knowing that it is the truth."

After this they pull out his tongue.

The executioners would have wished to do more to al-Hillaj, but the evening prayer time was at hand. So the mob of true believers pressed the torturers to cut off the heretic's head so they could go to the mosque and pray. As the sword came down, al-Hillaj flashed a loving, blood-soaked smile.

It was a smile that somehow rose through the sirocco dust devil of physical pain and surrounding violence from an unfathomable depth in the center of the cyclone.

There are many other stories of a peace that passeth understanding being the axle in a whirlwind life of suffering and persecution. In far more recent times, the Bahá'í prophet 'Abdul'l-Bahá lived in less physically harsh, but no less psychically crippling circumstances as an inmate in a Turkish prison cell.

At a lecture in Paris in 1911, 'Abdul'l-Bahá shared with an attentive crowd his secret for surviving incarceration.

"I myself was in prison forty years," he recalled. "One year alone would have been impossible to bear—nobody survived that imprisonment more than a year! But, thank God, during all those forty years I was supremely happy every day. On waking, it was like hearing good tidings, and every night infinite joy was mine. Spirituality was my comfort, and turning to God was my greatest joy. If this had not been so, do you think it possible that I could have lived through those forty years in prison?

"Thus spirituality is the greatest of God's gifts, and 'Life Everlasting' means 'Turning to God.' May you, one and all, increase daily in spirituality, may you be strengthened in all goodness, may you be helped more and more by the Divine consolation, be made free by the Holy Spirit of God, and may the power of the heavenly kingdom live and work among you."

Slightly more than a half-century later another controversial founder of a new religion was recorded on a prison video monitoring system. You could see him sitting in a feces-smeared jail cell in Charlotte, North Carolina, in 1985, seemingly undisturbed, sipping his water as if he were riding comfortably in one of his Rolls-Royces.

This was the same man who, as a young boy in Gadarwara, India, enjoyed jumping off a 60-foot-high railway bridge into the swirling, monsoon-swollen waters of a flooded river. Where other athletic adults had drowned, this slight lad happily navigated the strong currents and even allowed the river's notorious whirlpools to suck him down toward what could have been a silty, earth-brown death.

The boy didn't fight the current—he relaxed.

Such was the case if death came or not, he reasoned. Drowning in the river was preferable to drowning in a lifetime of fear.

The closer death came to him—knocking its arrival on his compressed lungs, pressing watery hands over his tightening throat—the more the boy simply gave in, surrendering himself to the current and into relaxation. Eventually he found his body circling around the center of the whirlpool's liquid tornado. There at its base, he discovered that the current is so weak that all one needed to do was step out of it and rise to the surface, alive and well.

The boy would grow up to become a professor of philosophy and eventually one of the late-twentieth century's most controversial Indian mystics. He would also gain inspiration from the poem of Rumi, and contribute the following interpretation:

"Rumi is saying: The news we hear is full of grief for the future. But the real news inside, is there's no news at all. Everything is silent and everything is as beautiful, peaceful, blissful as it has always been. There is no change at all; hence, there is no news.

"Inside is an eternal ecstasy, forever and forever.

"I will repeat again that these lines may become true in your lifetime. Before that happens, you must reach within yourself where no news has ever happened, where everything is eternally the same, where the spring never comes and goes but always remains; where the flowers have been from the very beginning—if there was any beginning—and are going to remain to the very end—if there is going to be any end. In fact, there is no beginning and no end, and the garden is lush, green and full of flowers.

"Before the outside world is destroyed by your politicians, enter into your inner world. That's the only safety left, the only shelter against nuclear weapons, against global suicide, against all the idiots who have so much power to destroy.

"You can at least save yourself." (Osho [1987] *The Hidden Splendor*)

CHAPTER TWO
The Unbearable Lightness
Of Being Ordinary

A man walked the earth, but there was no solid gold nimbus from an altar image weighing down upon his head. A man spoke a sermon on the mount, but there was no Cinemascope to widen the horizon. A man on a donkey rode into Jerusalem surrounded by a crowd with palm fronds. Alfred Newman, the legendary movie score composer, didn't magnify the emotional impact of the entry with a melodious chorale, and there was no Hollywood sound mixer to edit out the people singing off-key.

In the reenactment of this moment in Christ's life in the movie *The Robe*, there's a close-up shot of Victor Mature, who played a Greek slave on the roadside watching the man on the donkey pass by. The chorus suddenly stops its prancing song and the voices assume solemn hallowed tones that shiver and brighten along with the widening gleam of Mature's eyes as the passing donkey rider regards him off-camera. But in the actual historical event there was no manly Mature submitting like a timid doe frozen in the floodlights of a God-man's eyes. No orchestra and chorus were there to augment the donkey passenger's presence or ghetto-blast his aura with an angelic atmosphere that could raise God-sized goose bumps.

Everyone looks better in a movie adaptation. Buddha is sexy thanks to Keanu Reeve's portrayal in *Little Buddha*. Jesus looks like the John Wayne of messiahs because of Jeffrey Hunter's square-jawed Aryan looks in *King of Kings*. Over time you have to Charlton Heston your Hosanna. Even in Islam, a religion that frowns on any physical portrayal of the Prophet Muhammad, the actors and extras in the movie *The Message* regard him off-camera with respectful drop-jawed gapes.

The movies didn't start the trend. They are the most recent artistic collusion in the habit of deifying and distancing future followers from their saviors. The icons of Christ stare us down with flat and superhuman portraits. How can the sweaty and dusty man on the flea-bitten donkey match Michelangelo's clean, white, and unblemished marble facsimile of Jesus Christ in the Pietà? He lies draped forever in crucified ecstasy in the lap of his ageless mother of the immaculate marble face-lift. Countless statues of Buddha in perfect repose make it hard to imagine he ever stood with the wind, peeing in perfect repose like the rest of his monks. You never see Lord Krishna in his dirty underwear, and the cows and cowgirls he frolics with are always dung-free and sparkling clean.

A messiah's makeover makes sense. If Superman is the man of steel, saving the world, then my savior can't be just another four-eyed Clark Kent. Can I worship someone who's on my level? Can someone just as frail, reeking of garlic, and as faulty as myself rule over the world for a thousand years?

A mere political leader looks down at us from the dais; a simple priest or preacher stands high and mighty at the pulpit above his flock. How much more rarefied and otherworldly must be the returned world redeemer? My religious leaders teach me to obey a higher authority. Therefore it is only natural that I feel more inclined to submit myself to someone who is extraordinary. Whether the founder of my religion is a model of modesty or megalo-messianism, he must be either higher—or humbly lower—than I could ever be. He can't just be an ordinary man.

Mahavir, the 24th divinely incarnated master of Jainism and Buddha's contemporary, is said to have attained his God-manliness while squatting in a field in a yogic position called Milking the Cow. Let no one even suggest that Mahavir at that moment was also attaining another more basic and down-to-earth making form of *liberation.*

Ordinariness undermines all that is holier than thou. If extraordinary insight into the divine mystery can sprout from flea-bitten donkey riders and people pooping in a field—if enlightenment can make a superman out of every schlepp of a Clark Kent—then where is the need for anyone presuming religious hierarchy and extraordinariness over others? What religious hierarchy could keep dictating how we think and feel about godly redeemers if the truth got out that godliness was as everyday and normal as carrying water, fetching firewood, eating, breathing and defecating?

The Man Behind the God-Man Myth

I have met a few rare individuals who hid the whole sky in their eyes. They filled the atmosphere with the silent aura of their "ordinariness" melting my heart, babbling my brain. They had an extraordinary sense of relaxation. They were non-serious people, but profoundly sincere. I never felt judged in their presence, even though some of these people cut my ego to the quick with a passing remark, a giggle, or when they quietly ignored me when I was being needy. These people were adults—some were near my age, some were pushing 90—but where I was at times childish, they were ever childlike. To them, being ordinary was just like being innocent, open, fresh—and their intelligence seemed to capture the fragrance of youth and vitality, even if they were physically very old and infirm.

What they defined as ordinary were things I considered miraculous. For instance, they said it was natural and normal for a human being to live in the fulfillment of "effects" without needing a "cause." In other words, they didn't seek lovers, they were love; they didn't seek fulfillment, they came to understand that they were fulfillment itself. When others became abusive of them, they did not respond in kind with anger or crumple in victimhood. It was as if the poison rising in the abuser had no bridge to the abused, therefore there was no one abused. They didn't suffer the cyclone of life because they didn't identify with it.

But when I say this, don't think I mean they were renunciates, holier than thou, and high above the struggle of life. The mystics I have known loved life, and they lived it to the fullest. They danced, they made love, they enjoyed life's moods and its beauties, but they didn't seem to carry expectations.

To people of tremendous seriousness and importance, these mystics were unbearable. People wanted them to get caught up in their drama, and they just wouldn't behave. These mystics had *ignore-sense*, rather than ignorance. They seemed ever able to sniff out the truffles of truth from the forest floor of illusion. It was as if they saw something we didn't see, but *could* see if we just had the right sense to see it. It was as if these "ordinary" people—once colorblind like ourselves—had rediscovered how to see and celebrate life in full Technicolor.

They saw death in full color, too. In one case I watched one of these self-proclaimed "ordinary" men, Osho, blissfully face his approaching death over a six-month period. On the night of January 19, 1990, I helped take his body down to the burning ghats on an Indian river for cremation. The man faced death as he faced everything: in a state of "such is the case." He was not for it, he was not against it.

Things seem to meld together in the consciousness of such "ordinary" people. Where we see "love," they see "love/hate." Where we see "death," they see "death/life." Where I see irreconcilable opposites, the ordinary man sees complements.

Dr. Amrito, Osho's personal physician and my friend, related to me and other devotees his experience of Osho's final moments. On the last morning, Amrito said the body showed signs that Osho's heart was about to fail. He told me his patient nodded and spent the rest of the day making his final arrangements as if he were merely preparing for a weekend trip. At one point Amrito began to weep. The dying man looked at him, almost sternly—a rare expression for someone who was always so joyous. Osho frowned at the tears and said, "No, this is not the way." When my friend stopped crying, the "ordinary" man gave him the sweetest of loving smiles before he peacefully died.

Osho had a love of Rolls-Royces. When cornered by someone who disapproved of a religious man driving luxury cars, he shrugged a reply: "I *am* a simple man—I simply love the best."

This "simple" man also dressed in fantastic robes made by his female disciples. The robes were woven out of the finest fabrics, and often his knitted caps were ringed in rows of simply beautiful precious stones and pearls. When I was a resident in his commune in Oregon (1983-1986) and later when he returned to his ashram in Pune, India (1987-1990), I'd see him driving the cars and wearing a new expensive gown almost every day.

I have to admit that I was a bit skeptical about Osho's "ordinariness."

For skeptics such as myself, I am reminded of the following ancient Hindu fable Osho often told to help us understand his unique brand of ordinariness:

News reached an Indian maharaja that a famous sadhu (religious renunciate) had come to sit under a tree in his kingdom. The maharaja had heard so much about this mystic's spiritual transcendence of all illusion and worldly things that he drove his chariot over to visit him. He found the sadhu sitting under a tree, naked as a "Jain" bird, meditating in silent ecstasy.

Out of politeness, the maharaja invited the sadhu to come to his palace and enjoy its luxuries as his guest. Just as it was the social custom of the time for a maharajah to offer, it was the custom for the renunciate to lovingly refuse, to show his transcendence of the world.

The sadhu's eyes popped open, and he stood up and said, "Okay, let's go."

The naked man climbed onto the chariot and, grinning, motioned the stunned maharaja to have his driver whip the horses to a gallop for the palace.

Over the next few weeks the sadhu taught the maharajah about renunciation, meditation, and spiritual liberation while he happily sampled his best food, dressed in his beautiful robes, and enjoyed the company of the maharajah's most beautiful palace courtesans.

The maharajah sulked until he could stand it no longer. One day he found the mystic living the life of Lord Krishna, lounging on a divan enjoying the garden and its peacocks, while maidens lay at his feet serenading him with songs and sitars.

"You are a fraud! sputtered the maharajah "How can you call yourself a renunciate? A religious man should abandon worldliness."

The finely robed sadhu was unfazed. "I have been expecting this," he said. "Frankly, I am surprised at how long it took you to let fly your displeasure. So extraordinary are your ideas of what being religious is."

The sadhu hopped from the divan and began walking out of the garden. "Come on, bring your chariot, it is time for me to go."

The sadhu directed the maharajah to drive him to the edge of his kingdom. Once they reached the border, he descended from the chariot and gave back all the jewels and beautiful clothes until he was once again the epitome of a naked renunciate. He said good-bye and began to walk away.

Seeing him naked as the day they first met, the maharajah could sense the sadhu's spiritual aura, and he felt ashamed. He fell at his feet asking for forgiveness.

"Please return to my palace. Now I understand that you are indeed a holy man."

The sadhu stopped and turned around. "No, I will not return," he said firmly, but with kind eyes. "If I go back I will put on your robes, enjoy your food, and celebrate life with your ladies-in-waiting, and you will again feel that this man is a fraud. Then you will once again demand that I leave.

"My poor beloved friend, you cannot see the natural man before you. You only see your ideas of how a holy man should be. There is no need to renounce things. One only needs to renounce the attachment to things. I am free to enjoy everything—or nothing—because the source of my enjoyment is free of any cause or any effect. Therefore I can leave your place and be naked again in the wilderness. It doesn't matter, nor does it affect my liberation."

The day came when tragic events put the gist of this fable to the test.

In late October 1985, I remember one day seeing Osho in one of his fine caps and robes driving his Rolls-Royce slowly past a line of thousands of his adoring celebrating disciples. The next day I saw him on television after US federal agents arrested him, alone, sitting behind bars in faded and rough-woven prison dungarees. There was no car, no silken robe, no pearl-lined cap to cover his balding head, but I perceived that nothing had changed inside him. He was cool and relaxed. Now he was like the naked sadhu, but he exuded the same relaxed "such is the case" gaze he showed when richly attired.

I'm not saying he was enjoying being arrested. Rather, I'm saying that the arrest could not disturb his joy. His incarceration had cruel and unusual aspects. For one thing, the deferral marshals had arrested him without a warrant or a publicly announced indictment in a case that the US prosecutors later admitted they couldn't actually prove. When they jailed this aging, "ordinary" man, the federal marshals forced him to drag himself around in leg, wrist, and waist irons "for his protection."

About six months after Osho was deported from the United States—and it was clear that his commune had become Oregon's newest ghost town—the chief prosecutor of the case, Charles Turner, admitted in public and in print that the arrest was politically motivated, just to get the guru out.

Despite his ordeal, I recall Osho reflecting on his arrest, pointing out that even in the outwardly worst circumstances, a person can live in the suchness of their ordinary divinity and even make music "dancing to the clinking sound of your chains."

i-diocy the Empty Sky?
I struggle with the word *ordinary*

Applying this label to mystics like a Krishnamurti or an Osho seems so inadequate. The world "ordinary" is a boring, black-and-white word. It is Rice-a-Roni compared to gourmet Italian risotto. "Ordinary" is a clunky Trabant or a working-class Subaru when I want to drive an appellation that roars like a Corvette Sting-Ray or purrs like a Rolls-Royce Silver Spur sedan.

Well…what to do?

I'm not qualified to talk about being ordinary, because I am an extraordinary personality.

Or, putting it more bluntly, I am an idiot.

This Greek word comes from the root *idios*, which stands for "identity." An extraordinary life requires that I *I*-dentify with emotions, thoughts, and things. I am "John." I am an "American." I love this. I hate that. I hope, I fear, I do the *I*-diot.

Idios also means being "special" or "distinct" from other personalities. *I*-diocy is what you get when society seeds the empty skylike being of a child's soul with the dark rain clouds of a borrowed identity. Nevertheless, if one is aware, one sees that for any identification to exist, it requires its opposite. If society and religion can program you to *I*-dentify, there is a chance that you can deprogram yourself from religious and societal conditioning and experience dis-*I*-dentification. Society conditions us into ego personified through a hurricane of beclouded thoughts and feelings. But however dark and roiling this hurricane may be, it must rotate around a profoundly becalmed inner eye at its center. That eye in the idiot's storm can be a window to the larger sky we have forgotten. It is a reminder of the unbearable lightness of being infinite.

A spiritual master is like that endless sky.

You and I are also that sky, but there's a difference. Every moment, waking or sleeping, a master is the eternal remembrance of what we keep forgetting.

In an ever-empty sky the storm clouds of hate and fear may froth and curl and exhaust their rage, while at other times love clouds of delightful sunrise and sunset colors dance, but behind all the nice and nasty cloud-play—sky.

A spiritual master is a sky that remembers itself.

You and I are a sky that forgets, and identifies with the clouds.

Now, what if a spiritual teacher, remembering the "skyness" of being, felt a compassion to convey that "remembrance" to other *parts* of the sky, parts that only exist with a false context. Parts of the sky still caught up in identification with clouds?

How will that empty sky communicate its awakening to the beclouded sky?

What language will it use?

Certainly it cannot expect the beclouded sky to understand cloudless communication. The empty sky will have to speak the other's language. It will have to wax foggy. The empty sky will have to wear a mask—maybe even a cumulonimbus-sized mask of a messiah.

Communication cannot by definition be one-side. For even if the beclouded sky can become a disciple, it must wonder if there is more to those rare blue holes that disturb the overcast topography of its personality. Toward such overclouded skies the cloudless master calls, wearing a nebulous mask. The master approaches, enticing the beclouded sky to become its disciple. Then the master shows this disciple infinitesimal glimpses of the blue vault of liberation beyond its cumulus mask. The disciple doesn't understand but is intrigued, and wants to see more holes in the gray gloom of its life.

The empty sky, as a master, must be careful not to reveal too much of its burning blueness all at once. The disciple still thinks the master is there to make the halos in the translucent cloud-forms brighter and more spiritual, when the master is really a thief from the cloudless night, working to dispel all the disciple's misty illusions

The disciple believes itself to be the clouds.

The master knows the disciple is the sky itself.

The master must tread cautiously, or the disciple will see too soon where this emptiness leads—to complete evaporation of its cloudy raison d'être. If the disciple isn't ready to see the *all*, it will retreat deeper into the cloud-illusion.

The empty, clear sky is patient. Over time the sky-master mixes more holes of its true blueness into the cloudy bait and the cumulonimbus-savior promises.

The disciple over time becomes acquainted with existence beyond the low, middle, and high-level clouds of its identification, until there comes a moment when the fabulous voice is yawning wide enough through the clouds for the disciple to finally understand there is no master. There is no disciple, either. They were formlessness sustaining the form-play of idiotic clouds.

There is only one sky.

If our great teachers down through history are guilty of playing along with some of our messiah myths and salvation expectations, they did it because we were unable to see their ordinariness with our extraordinary and idiotically cloudy perceptions. Still, those few who understand what is hidden from most of us will continue to persuade us to follow them as our guides to enlightenment. They are not our saviors as such—they are fellow travelers. They are friends who have traveled a little farther down the road than you or me. That's all.

To heed the call to follow a friend like the Galilean or the Buddha takes but one small hole of blue memory disturbing an idiot's overcast soul.

After that, it takes guts, a capacity to celebrate everything, and unconditional trust.

The Path of Trust

The word *Guru* is a new victim in the serial killing of beautiful words by pop-culture. Apply it in titles like "guru of golf," or the "gurus of Washington wonk" and you have secularized this Hindu term for a religious teacher to fit any Svengali of politics, sports or the arts. The technically correct dictionary translation of the Sanskrit word "guru" is the "venerable one" or "the spiritual master," but that definition is a dead statue to anyone who has known and loved the real living and breathing article. The seeker touched by the presence of the guru knows a far more poetic definition.

A guru is like a great cloud, heavy with rains. So burdened is the rain cloud that it cannot contain itself. The heavy cloud must give the rain to the earth. The guru cloud doesn't put conditions on where it deposits its rains; the guru cloud will equally share its bountiful showers on the sterile rocks and the fertile,   thirsty   soil. A guru is a giving phenomenon.

A guru drowns its parched recipient with a monsoon of love, a cloudburst of refreshing awareness.

A guru doesn't do anything. Just as the cloud doesn't decide when or upon whom it releases its showers, a guru releases the heavy, bountiful silence and peace of his presence on everyone. And as with the rain, most people will just "open their umbrellas" and ignore this intrusion, while a precious few find the "soaking" to the marrow inspiring.

In this latter group are the people who seek out gurus. They gather around the guru's tranquil eye in the center of a cyclone that is an *ashram*—the guru's spiritual community, or college campus of seekers and disciples; or, call it a meditation resort of the last resort. Dozens or tens of thousands of disciples can surround the guru of an ashram, and it can appear to outsiders and followers alike that he is their leader. It can appear that he is doing something to influence them. But a guru is not a doer. You could say he is filled to the brim with *being*.

Is-ness is his business.

The rain cloud doesn't make an effort to grow flowers. Let the flowers and the rocks respond as they like. They are the doers. The rock does the drying off and forgets the rain; the seeded earth does the blossoming.

A guru is a catalytic agent. He or she precipitates a process in disciples without being involved in or changed by the consequences. He may walk and sit and eat and do the things other people do. He may help precipitate a transformation in his disciples as a result of committing some action that might surprise and shock the disciple to attention. A guru can be like a thunderclap—a rain cloud thunders whether or not anyone is there to be jolted to attention. The doing—or lack of response—to the Guru's thunder is up to the disciple.

Each seeker of a spiritual teacher must bear witness to this mystery in their own unique way. I can say from my own experience with Osho that you know you are in the presence of an authentic guru when just his presence, his silence, is enough to bring new context to your existence. Just the fragrance of the master's "Is-ness" can resurrect a forgotten knowing. Just his aura of no-worry, no-body-ness can nourish new buds of a lost innocence sprouting in a life lived in the drought-cracked land of society's conditioning.

The guru is full of an emptiness you once had: a cleanness of mind and spirit you had forgotten. The guru is a catalytic agent for remembrance of a time when your brain wasn't a dustbin for other people's ideas and emotional baggage.

The master's call is like the first kiss of humidity against the cracked and desiccated land. It is the electricity in the dry season's stifling heat preceding the guru thunderstorm. You are expectant like the land. You trust that wet kiss on your cracked and desertlike face more than all the so-called better judgment dumped into you by your society's mentors and tormentors. Something magnetic awakens inside and it draws you to his presence. Your heart leads the way, dragging the ego along like a cluster of cans clattering behind a honeymoon carriage. You go to the guru dragging your rusty bits of better judgment, ideas of love, and mental training along for the ride.

You go to your master. You take a risk.

Maybe society is right, and your guru is indeed a madman like a Hitler, or Jim Jones, or an Asahara. Still you gamble that this one will not exploit you for his or her own messianic ego trip. You put your trust in your guru as being God's madman, or as Godliness itself wearing a persona or masquerading in a brief illusion of form as a fly lure for the Infinite Fisherman to catch your heart.

Once it becomes clear that you have, for better or worse, already thrown your "deity dice" on this person's crap table, you become your master's disciple—you become someone willing to learn. This is fifty percent of the journey down the path of trust. In the second half the guru helps you take two more steps on the path.

STEP ONE:
The Master Becomes your Deprogrammer
And Your Inspiration to Experiment

Real trust has no conditions attached. A real guru is an inspiration, not an enslaver. He nurtures a trust in experimentation, rather than nourishing your blind belief. An authentic master won't give you a belief to follow. A messiah like Adolf Hitler demands blind belief. A real master strives to make you aware of many unconscious pathologies that keep you unblissfully unaware of your true nature. You know you are in the presence of a real guru when you find all your expectations exposed while living with him. If you don't let them go they will be, figuratively speaking, rubbed in your face.

Usually incidents with other disciples reveal your ego trips in the day-to-day affairs of life in the master's spiritual community. At the same time, a real ashram also gives you a safe haven for going through what are often painful revelations, because you can see that you are not alone. Everyone's ego trips are being exposed there. Also, you feel encouraged to look deeper into yourself because you see how many around you are becoming happier and more integrated human beings.

The ashram is a hard place for ego trips to sustain themselves, but it is a garden that nourishes one's rise to clarity and happiness. Being a member of a real master's community of disciples doesn't make you dependent or turn you into a spiritual slave. If at first he requires you to surrender to him and to the regimens of his ashram, it is no more unreasonable than a surgeon asking you to remain on the operating table until he finishes the operation.

It takes great intelligence to surrender yourself to a guru. He can say or do something outrageous, even unjustified, but if something he says or does as a device causes you to leave his presence in the middle of the operation, you are the loser. You have chosen trifles over transcendence. The master doesn't care about being politically or religiously correct, he cares about *you*. He wants to upset all your judgment ducks, set in a neat row by your society. He has the compassion to poke a stick into the spokes of your finely tuned morality. He's there to show that both good judgments and bad are worthless if they are borrowed.

A true master wants to destroy the chains connecting you to all arranged marriages with hand-me-down knowledge. He wants to pull the plug on your past and short out your fossilized traditions. He's out to turn off your ego's TV so the empty screen will reflect the couch potato pundit that idiotic life has made you. A master holds up a mirror to your face, risking his life for you, because most people don't want to see their true reflection. They can break the mirror, persecute, and even kill, its holder. A true disciple, however, may cringe at the image of himself or herself, yet be grateful that the master cared enough to show the reflection of an adopted persona—a mask—no matter how ugly it may be. If someone doesn't expose the mask, how can you take it off and see your original face?

In the first step toward becoming unbearably light with ordinary being, the master is your surgeon. Sometimes the operation to relieve you from conditioned habits and borrowed identities is as painful as peeling off your own skin. The "honeymoon" with the guru may be over, yet one who is willing to learn must trust the mysterious doctor. You must follow the instructions of the master-midwife and bear down on the waves of contractions as you give birth to your own lost understanding of who you really are. And the skin he's peeling is the rough hide of ego. It's not real. It's not *you*. The master takes nothing from you that is Truth. Only the false falls to his scalpel.

After the cathartic work is finished, the master's next job is to pose experiments that the disciples must test for themselves. In my own case, my master admonished me gently but firmly to always remember that if during self-observation I dislike what I see coming up out of my unconscious, then face it. If I want to avoid something in life—never avoid. When fear stands up to paralyze me—go into that fear.

"That's the only way to finish it," Osho said, "otherwise it will haunt you like a shadow."

Anger, greediness for this and that, fears, pride, phoniness, etc.—name your worst nightmares from the ID (your IDiot nightmare), then see them come at you like demons. Don't shrink back. Do exactly the opposite of what your society's conditioning says you should or should not do. In my case, I faced—and still face—my demon programs. The ego, when faced straight-on rather than avoided or repressed, simply vanishes. I watch these programs as my master instructed, without judgment for or against, mindful of my breath, relaxing. What is watched isn't "my" thoughts and feelings, they are "the" thoughts and feelings, passing in and out. They are mental traffic on the mind's freeway, and I'm sitting by the side of the road. Sometimes the freeway is empty; sometimes there's a traffic jam of thoughts and emotions. The trick is not to get caught in the traffic, but just to watch the "cars" go by. Let the cars of thought honk and weave and fender-bend after their own destinations. Putting it another way, my being—my "watcher"—is like the sky. There is a "seeing" of clouds floating by—puffy, white, and smiling, or dark and thunderous—across empty sky.

A real master doesn't want you to believe his or her statements, Belief to a true master is a cuddly euphemism that masks a state of blind ignorance. A master teaches you to either know something as your own experience, or to accept all that is unknown. Above all, he lays before a disciple the hypothesis that you can celebrate everything—happiness, sadness, life, death, all of it. He teaches acceptance of yourself, of others, even acceptance of non-acceptance.

A master will tell you often that he is just an ordinary human being, like you. He's no messiah or God-man or Avatar come to take up your sins or your responsibilities.

He'll say you don't need saving. You need "waking."

That's the only small difference between you and the master. You are extraordinarily sleepwalking through life, and he is ordinarily awake.

Once a sleepwalker, now an awakened one, the master will declare, "If I can wake up, so can you."

STEP TWO:
Gratefulness, No-Knowing

It has been 37 years and counting that I've been testing my master's experiments, and I haven't really figured out anything. In the beginning I had many questions. When my master responded, he didn't answer them as such; it was as if he made my questions vanish. Over time the clouds of questions slowly disappeared and left behind just a sky made of *answer*.

Not all of his hypotheses agreed with me, but that was not a problem. My master always encouraged me to follow my own way, to celebrate being as equally unique a human being as he was. If something didn't work, it only meant that we still needed to find techniques in meditation or therapies that harmonized with my individuality. The essential hypothesis Osho suggested to me was that ultimately existence itself is the teacher.

Life is the master.

When I also discovered this through my own experimentation, I began to see the master's sutures of insight slowly become my own.

Thus I began to understand the second step a disciple takes with a master. You begin to experience union with him or her. In the beginning you fall into a rhythm with the master as your most cherished beloved, but it is not a romantic affair of soulmates. The one-on-one coupling I've shared with women in this life, as rich and fulfilling as it has been, is nothing compared with the disciple-master relationship. It is one-ego-on-no-ego. It is one *I*-diot in love with a Nobody. It is a one-on-zero affair. You are somebody. You are trying to be something, whereas the master is no-thing being. And there's the mysterious paradox. He is full of this emptiness, he is a monsoon cloud bursting with rain, and like rain his emptiness nourishes a thirsty soul. Even the pitter-patter of his showers on the roof of your resistance is comforting to you.

The master is an empty void that has a bright awareness about it. You feel that he has arrived. Yet he is a vacant, non-present presence. A body walks up to you and talks to you. A man dances with you, but even though the body is total and animated in its moves, it appears just as empty as a corpse. You dance with him and become aware that this corpse is far more alive than you. It is as if the sky decided one day to hide inside the shell of a human body so it could relate to you and love you. The only hint of the sky's masquerade is the bright and penetrating emptiness of his eyes.

You find yourself falling in love with zero. It is like the legend of the great lovers, Tristan and Isolde. They adored each other with such intensity that they both disappeared into that love. They became so aware of love that they became love. Love liberated them from being egos, from being limited in time or confined in sexually identified minds and bodies. They became love's eternity, love's endless sky. In the same way, by staying close to the master you begin to disappear into his state of union and non-separation. Tasting his no-thing-ness, your starved soul begins to become wet with his nectar. Once this has happened, once the master gets his emptiness under your skin, his physical existence becomes irrelevant. The sky was not the body. It was just visiting you. You are not the body either. In those moments when the master merged with you, he showed you that you are also the sky hiding behind form.

To merge with a master is called *Satsang*. There is no appropriate translation in any Western language for this Sanskrit word. I can say this, from my own experience: Satsang happens when you come close to a master, so close that his emptiness helps you to dissolve into "it." Suddenly, unexpectedly, you disappear into his whole in the clouds. The mind and all its thoughts falls away; the emotions and all their turbulence of hurts and expectations vanish. You become light and lightning-bright with the same focusless attention of the master. Satsang is a coupling. He has disappeared and so have you. For a moment there is no master, no disciple. No-thing.

At this juncture prose must be left behind. The language of books is a language of the *coulds* and *shoulds* of the idiots; its expression is extraordinary. Language separates, distinguishes. Words and sentences are like Tristan-and-Isolde egos before they dissolved into no-ego. Language dissects the flower of a master-disciple union into its parts. Language divides and dismantles the mystic flower of Satsang until it lies in pieces on the floor, killed. The only way to understand what I'm saying is to find a master, sit with him or her and disappear into his love and awareness.

A look with no intention.
A robe of green, fluttering,
> like a poplar tree sage in a desert.

A moonlight leaf,
> causing the cockerel to purr
> in the almond tree.

The hum held in your hands,
The eyes wide-open gazing backwards
> at something beyond the seen:

> The one you recognize in me.

A rocking moves my frame from nowhere,
> and meeting draws closed our eyes.

And you never saw me.
And I never saw you.

> So that we could *re-member*.

Through moments of Satsang with my master I have tasted the essence of the opening, the lifting veil, Mystic-Rose *Apocalypse* of the Awakened Ones. As far as I understand it, this is one of their secrets: no messiah as such is coming to save us. The savior sleeps within each of us.

Worship not the awakened mystics. Understand them as the reflections of your own divine potential. Their physical sojourn on this earth is an invitation to ignite the fire of your sleeping consciousness. To indicate this truth, they led you from the periphery of the outer apocalypse to the untapped majesty hiding *within*.

"In that moment there is no Master, no disciple," explains Osho. "Just two flames have come so close to each other, they have become one flame.

"The disciple starts smelling of the same fragrance as the Master. His eyes start showing the same raw light as the Master. His vibe becomes the same as the Master.

"And then the tremendous gratitude: the gratitude that this man did not give me a belief, otherwise I was lost. This man did not make me dependent on him, otherwise I am lost. This man did not exploit me psychologically in any way, for his own ego, otherwise I would not have been able even to find what is happening.

"Because I was sick, I was needful, he could have easily exploited my needs for his own ego. He could have created the vicious circle of fulfilling the ego: you fulfill the Master's ego, the Master fulfills the disciple's ego." (Osho [1984] *From Misery to Enlightenment*)

Many Candles—One Flame

In the new Aquarian Age, the individual's spiritual journey will be nurtured by the cumulative impact of millions of other individuals seeking enlightenment on an unprecedented scale. This global wave of spiritual seeking will occur, say the more rebellious prophets and mystics, only after individuals break free from the shackles of greed for heaven, fear of hell, and all the other life-negative dogmas of the dying religions of the closing Piscean Age.

The new dispensation will also free the enlightened master from the shackles of messianism. As we abandon our myths about saviors, those upon whom we have projected that myth will find themselves liberated from their masks such as God-man, Avatar, Messiah, Twelfth Imam, or Redeemer. When at last we see their original faces, these individuals will simply become our teachers, our friends.

If one candle can light millions, the flame of one awakened human being can light millions of unlit souls.

"One day when you come REALLY close to a master, something jumps from the master into you - a flame. Just as it happens when you bring an unlit candle very close to a lit candle. Just a moment before, the unlit candle was unlit and the lit candle was lit. And just a moment afterwards, at a certain distance the flame jumps and both the candles are lit. And the lit candle has not lost anything, and the unlit has gained all

"The master never loses anything. That's why millions of disciples can become lit through a single master." (Osho [1978] *Take It Easy Vol 2*)

"Once you have tasted your own immortality, you start spreading an invisible fire...no intellectual argument, but people will be immensely touched by your very presence, by your aroma, by your fragrance, by your love. We need in the world more love to balance war." (Osho [1987] *The New Dawn*)

CHAPTER THREE
The Buddhafield

"Just as death faces an individual, similarly death shows its dark face before the collective consciousness of an entire civilization. And that civilization's collective mind becomes ready to go deep into the realms of religion and the unknown… This can repeat itself again; there is a complete possibility for it. (Osho [1971] *Dimensions Beyond the Known*)

"Never before was the search so acute, so intense, because never before was man in such an anguish as he is today. The search always comes out of anguish. Whenever there is great anguish, the anguish becomes a challenge, one has to search for something which is so meaningful that the anguish can be dissolved through it. When the darkness is very very deep, only then does one search for light. And the darkness is really deep. This is one of the darkest ages: never before has man been in such a disturbed, confused chaos. Because all the old values have disappeared. Man is no more rooted in the past, there are no more any goals in the future, all utopias have failed. Man is utterly desperate now to know what to do and where to go.

"In the past it has happened many times that a certain value became valueless, another value took its place, it was substituted. One religion died, another took its place. One idealism was found futile, another better vision, more golden, was immediately available. What has happened this time is that all the ideals have failed and there is no more any substitute. It is not that one value has failed and another has come into being: that is not much of a change. This time, value as such has failed and there is utter darkness, nowhere to go. This is the greatest challenge to human awakening. Hence I say, for the first time in history, the time is right for a great Buddhafield." (Osho [1978] *Let Go!*)

The Aquarian Age will see humanity take a quantum leap beyond what we currently know and believe. It will not be an era of father-figure gods sending their only begotten children to be persecuted and to preach salvation. It may see the end of messiahs as we have known them. They could be replaced by what many Aquarian Age prophets have foreseen as a "Christ" or "Buddha" force field. The savior of the twenty-first century could be a collective spiritual environment generated by thousands of awakening individuals who in turn were launched on their inner journey of self-discovery by one enlightened fellow traveler as their catalytic agent. Consequently, as more individual seekers gather together, they nourish this force field of collective awakening and intensify its presence and blissful vitality. This in turn attracts many more individual spiritual seekers into its ambiance.

Thus, the momentum created by so many individuals working and meditating to free themselves from the distortions of the past could create a field of energy that turns human destiny in a new direction, away from destruction and toward a life-affirming new era. Many prophets of this future potential foresee the arrival of a paradise on Earth 250 to 700 years from now—that is, if the Buddhafield is allowed to spread its presence across the world.

Escaping the Misery Field

Most of us live life in a "misery field." There are moments of love, brief encounters with happiness, and all-too-short plateaus of fulfillment. For the rest of our lives we endure a spiritual climate that is generally negative. The daily grind draws most of our creative energy into the whirlwind of competition for money, food, and prestige. The struggle to survive against competitors dominates most of our day, from the nuclear family level all the way up to the family of nations. The things have become more valuable than the people themselves. In the richer misery fields you are your car, your lace bra—your secrets are Victoria's Secret. You are your job.

In a culture of misery, life must be a hell to make heaven more appealing. No wonder popes as recently as the beginning of the twentieth century were declaring social progress in world democracy a vehicle of Satan. The children brought into this misery biosphere soon see their bright and questioning beings dulled. The children of each generation learn how to be miserable through their lifetime conditioning in the three Rs: Rote education, Robotic belief, and Regret.

You know you are lost in a misery field when laughter is a disturbance, when duty dulls the divine innocence, when burdens become virtues. People cellphone-selfie their lives rather than live them. Memories are always sweet because the present situation in a misery field always sucks. You know misery rules when people can't be alone and will compromise themselves to live in dysfunctional families and marriages. They will surrender to the will of national bodies, and sell their souls to religious pathologies.

Stillness and silence irritate the ambiance of a misery field. Even in places where talk is obviously not necessary, people must cluck and fuss. For instance, on Super Bowl Sunday in January 1999, I hiked to the summit of Mt. Si in Washington State. The sun colored the snow powder, marbling the cracks in a 300-foot outcropping known as "the haystack" as if it had veins of golden filament. Above the haystack ice clouds lined up like celestial celebrants twirling in a cirrus dervish dance in an unfathomable blue sky. The pine trees, wearing their snowy-white mime faces, sighed in the wind. I planted my boots knee-deep in a snowdrift and hugged the scene with my being, my senses pressed against the still wonder like naked newlyweds.

Soon there were others reaching the vista, huffing and puffing and chattering about this and that. Until the others arrived, the vista point and I enjoyed a brief interlude away from the world's misery field. The new people brought their mental static with them even though the miracle of sun and snow-play upon rock and tree continued.

"Look, Mildred, golly it's sure cold up here...Brush that snow off or you'll get cold...Oh! That's pretty...Yep, but not as pretty as the last time...*blah, blah...* My hands are getting cold... Why didn't you put on those extra glove liners like I told you? ...Ah, you never listen to me, serves you right...Hey, Bob? Quick get a picture of it before the clouds come back... *blah, blah...* I'm hungry... *blah, blah...* Okay, let's get down in time to see the Super Bowl...*blah, blah, blah...*"

They jabbered while Mt. Si and I communed in silence. Even with all the chatter going on, the others sneaked suspicious glares at me for not blabbing along with them. My silence was politically incorrect.

At that moment I was more than a dropout, I was a step-out, an ecstatic. *Ecstasy* is the ancient Greek word for a state of extreme and intense sensitivity when one has suddenly exited from the world of the mundane.

It is not easy to keep a childlike sense of ecstasy alive in this world. When you are out in public, allow a relaxation into blissfulness without a "cause" and see how self-conscious you become. See how out of step you are. Note the fearful looks of some and the mean-spirited putdowns of others. See how something like a lead weight drags down your blissfulness once you allow it to emerge and be. The self-consciousness ends when your eyes resume the same dullness of the crowd and your body language assumes the plodding disposition of everyone else. It is at such moments when you return to the fold that you sense the worldwide thought field that keeps people down.

We are trained to generate it. It isn't anyone's fault, it is everyone's affliction, learned from cradle to corporation to crypt. The majority of us move through life in the misery field's automatic gear. Yet a handful of us over the centuries slip out of gear. Some of those who don't fit become religious seekers. Later on we mistake a handful of these misfits as our messiahs and avatars.

The mystically inclined have always required a spiritual retreat away from the magnetic influence of the misery-field worldliness. It is not by accident that there are monasteries far from the madding crowds. Spiritual seekers look for an oasis in the misery and violence of every era. They come out of the desert to drink at the well of a sacred place. They leave the noisy cities. They abandon the well-traveled roads. They wander off into nature, into the mountains, into the Himalayas. They appear antisocial when they are really anti-misery.

Where people locked in the misery field may collectively project a myth of off-world salvation and an escape into the clouds, there are those among us who seek a "Rapture" away from the world's loveless and negative thought field.

The Coming of the Transpersonal Messiah
"A great, unheard-of experiment has to be done, on such a large scale that at least the most substantial part of humanity is

touched by it—at least the soul of humanity, the center of humanity, can be awakened by it. On the periphery, the mediocre minds will go on sleeping—let them sleep—but at the center where intelligence exists a light can be kindled.

"The time is ripe, the time has come for it. My whole work here consists in creating a Buddhafield, an energy-field where these eternal truths can be uttered again. It is a rare opportunity. Only once in a while, after centuries, does such an opportunity exist...don't miss it!" (Osho [1979] *The Dhammapada: The Way of the Buddha*)

Whereas many people once or twice a year seek the peace and solitude of a vacation on an empty tropical beach, the few mystics of every generation take a somewhat different approach. They strive to create an alternative lifestyle, one where the spiritual vacation from the world never ends but deepens. It deepens so profoundly that even though the vacationer might return to the hurly-burly of the marketplace, he or she will not be *of* the marketplace. Instead the vacationer can become a center of cool and silent bliss in the cyclone of the misery field.

The mystics not only teach us that thoughts are a form of radiation, but that a higher state of "no-thought" can permeate a spiritual community and be like mists of a waterfall refreshing the surrounding forest with its healing presence. If fear and hate can haunt a place, so can love and compassion. The cumulative effect of silent, watchful minds and balanced, peaceful hearts can figuratively refresh the collective human spirit, enliven individual trees in the forest called *humanity*, and glisten the rocks of religious tradition with a new energy field.

In the last year before the new millennium, three pyramids of obsidian black reflected the South Asian sky and loomed over groves of scarlet-flowered flame trees and blue jacarandas in the Koregaon Park neighborhood of Pune, India. Below the canopy of trees, shaded from the Indian sun, you could see thousands of men and women from every race, dressed in maroon robes, coursing along the pedestrian thoroughfares of a multi-acre campus.

The people wove through a network of buildings of modern, even avant-garde, construction. Many structures were once sprawling bungalows and mansions built during the days of the British Raj, but all the buildings were repainted and marbled in black, with their windows tinted an iceberg blue. The contrast of the black buildings against the rivers of maroon-robed thousands and the surrounding subtropical gardens and forest canopy was strikingly beautiful rather than intimidating.

This is the Osho International Commune, currently called the Osho International Meditation Resort. It is today's largest buddhafield community experiment. It continues to be one of the world's greatest magnets for seekers and meditators. Over a million visitors have passed through the commune's Gateless Gate since it was established in the mid-1970s.

When night darkens the sky, robes of white replace the maroon robes of the people living there and visiting the resort. When I was last there in the spring of 2001, we proceeded down the thoroughfares of marble, illuminated by the glass columns over emerald-green lights, on our way to Buddha Hall. At that time it was a great dome, three stories high, made of arched girders and tent canvas that covered one acre in the center of the 32-acre campus since 1987. In 2001, the podium had upon it an empty chair.

Throughout the decades men and women filed inside to sit cross-legged in rows on a vast polished marble floor for discourses in Buddha Hall at the feet of Osho during the 1970s up to 1981 when we called him Bhagwan Shree Rajneesh ([*Bhagwan*] The Blessed One, [*Shree Rajneesh*] the Lord of the

Full Moon). In the early days the discourses were in the morning. We sannyasins (disciples) wore orange and red shades of the sunrise, yet over time, and after Osho returned from America to Buddha Hall in 1987, the robe "device" had been discarded for lovely street clothes at nightly discourses.

In the final years Osho asked us to wear maroon robes while inside the commune during the day and don white robes for the evening meeting that he named the White Robe Brotherhood. And thus we sat with him, backs straight, unmoving, as flutes and sitars caressed the air. We waited expectantly for someone who would never arrive—who was never born (nor ever died—so we devotees say), who was just a visitor from the formless playing for a brief 58 years in the form of our beloved master, who in the final months of his life we called *Osho*.

It's a Zen salutation used lovingly by disciples when addressing their beloved master. You might say it is a cosmic way of reverently saying "Sir." Before taking up the name, Bhagwan commented on William James' definition of "Osho" at least 11 times in his printed and recorded discourses in a way one might surmise that *Osho* was synonymous with "the Oceanic" consciousness. However when Bhagwan took the name, the definition was explained officially as this: "Osho" is a term derived from ancient Japanese, and was first used by Eka, to address his master, Bodhidharma.

"*O* means *with great respect, love and gratitude* as well as *synchronicity* and *harmony*. *Sho* means *multidimensional expansion of consciousness* and *existence showering from all directions*."

To the very end of his "visit" to this world, he would enter the hall as the music, dancing and clapping of thousands in a sea of white reached its peak and he would dance with us, suddenly freezing with his hands raised high over his head. We would lift our arms and a thunderous wave of sound would call his new name, "Osho!!!"

You could hear it echo throughout Koregaon Park like a wave disappearing into a profound silence it left behind.

Osho would begin dancing again and do this "stop" meditation a number of times before sitting in the richly upholstered white chair on the marble podium. On 10 April 1989 the discourses ended. His health had been rapidly worsening since he was arrested on US Federal counts for immigration fraud that the Federal justice system could never prove. Federal agents had arrested him without a warrant on rather flimsy and never-proven charges of immigration fraud and held him for 12 days in the US prison "gulag" system, shuttling him around various prisons by air. For three of those 12 days his lawyers lost track of where he was, government operatives poisoned Osho's food with a heavy metal agent, Thallium, which hasted his death from diabetes and heart disease by January 1990. All of Osho's symptoms that arose in the next four years were classic for the CIA's assassination weapon of choice that made him age 20 years in four.

In his final months (April 1989 to January 1990) he would come to the White Robe Fellowship when his strength allowed, as blissful in his greetings as ever. We would meet him each night in the assembled throng of Buddha Hall with great celebration and dancing as before. Osho would come in dancing as best he could, the "Oshos!" would reverberate, and then he'd sit in silence as we closed our eyes and hummed for 15 to 20 minutes. After that he would rise, fold his hands blessing us and slowly leave the hall, lifting them before departing for several stop meditations with a thunderous yell of "Osho!!!" from the thousands in white. We would remain sitting to a recording of his earlier discourses for another hour.

The last night Osho came into Buddha Hall. You can see it on YouTube.

(Copy this link in your browser:)
https://www.facebook.com/osho.international.meditation.resort/.

If you can't find it just search for it under the video title "I Leave You My Dream."

He was radiant as ever, and we were a white robed ocean, dancing, crying, and celebrating greater than ever before. The empty chair that sat between the two air conditioners had been removed so we could place Osho's bier and lay his radiant body prone upon them. I was there. I watched Osho's final meeting in Buddha Hall from beyond the mosquito nets behind the podium. I was picked to be on guard detail. I had been a former watchman at his house. We would ring the pallbearers for crowd control while they took his body to the nearby burning ghats at the riverside.

There are brief moments where I appear in this video, at the head of the procession as one of the guards helping to gently direct thousands of disciples aside to let his body through. For those readers and journalists who want confirmation that I was a witness to these events, check out minute 7:41-44. I'm near the upper left-hand corner edge of the video. You can see me turn my head back and forth once.

When, the body of Osho had been brought into Buddha Hall for its final farewell on the evening of 19 January 1990, several thousand white-robed followers danced and celebrated in front of the flower-festooned bamboo bier, in the most unusual and happiest funeral I have ever experienced. There were certainly a lot of tears but even in the midst of grief, most of the faces in that hall were filled with a glow of gratitude and love for a man who for them was the most remarkable person they had ever known and loved.

After ten minutes the body was carried off on its final journey to the burning ghats, the simple funerary crematoriums one finds along Indian rivers. Chance would have it that I walked alongside his body all the way to the ghats and because of the pressing crowds stayed next to the fire all night until the dawn broke. In the next three days and nights I took turns guarding one of the four corners of the burning pit. On the third morning I was guarding when his ashes were collected and walked back in an urn, held by his eldest brother, Vijay, where they would be laid in the Chuang Tzu auditorium that had been converted into his Samadhi—a master's resting place, around which disciples could meditate.

Escorting the bier to the ghats I could see him perfectly. Osho didn't look dead at all. Now I understand the stories about Zen disciples who resisted burning their master's body until they were sure he was really dead and not just playing a prank. Osho was just lying there. Very transparent, delicate, as if he were glowing from the inside. He was the most alive corpse I had ever seen. I couldn't believe he was actually dead until one of the pall bearers got a little carried away by the energy of the celebration just for a brief moment and his dancing gait made Osho's head and neck bob from side-to-side like rubber.

There were 2,000 to 5,000 people in white at the ghats. Still guarding, I stood in the first row gently asking people not to press closer. When the crowd had settled I sat there until dawn, so close to Osho's burning body that my face and hands the day after looked like they had been sunburned. Before the fire was lit I was very close to the final preparation of setting up the funeral pyre. I must have been next to the videographer because my memory of my last sight of Osho's peaceful face bathed in electric torches in a pit made of wood was just like what you see in the video as the final logs and flowers were lowered on to the funeral pyre. This was performed to the sounds of musical instruments and thousands of voices singing a stirring devotional song. The verses warmed the cold and humid Indian winter night air with the words, "Step into the holy fire, walk into the holy flame, oh! Halleluiah! Halleluiah!!"

Soon a great flame leapt up from the funeral pyre and all danced, sang and celebrated. Osho's family was to my right. They were crying like children. His younger brother Amit, in particular, was sobbing with such innocence and beauty that I was carried into his sobs. But even as the tears came I sensed a presence, a heresy, growing inside me over the next three days and nights that I was on my final watch as one of his watchmen and women.

"What are you crying for?" said the heresy (as if it could speak).

I felt I was saying goodbye to someone who hadn't left—couldn't leave me. For the rest of the night and up to the third and final morning afterwards when I sat at my watch on one of the corners of the pit before dawn until the time came to recover his ashes, this heresy grew, and along with thousands of other sannyasins, I could not contain my delight.

Osho often told his disciples that upon his death "I will dissolve into my people" in what he called the Buddhafield, the next stage in the evolution of human consciousness. This is a collective experience of enlightenment, an atmosphere of "Isness" into which all equally unique individuals can draw.

The days when people give up their responsibility to saviors are ending. Rather than the arrival of a Messiah in the twenty-first century, Osho predicted more of a collective awakening, or impersonal messianic experience. In other words, the Messiah is not coming—he is already hiding under our false egos and programmed behavior. The Messiah is within. Osho once said to Kurt Braun, the author of *Rajneeshpuram: The Unwanted Society*, that his people would become his autobiography.

Each night, at 7:00 pm, ever since Osho last physically came to greet us, a sea of thousands of white-robed men and women cover a marble floor before a podium topped by a richly upholstered white chair. The celebration music intensifies and the White Robe Brotherhood begins dancing and singing. For 30 minutes a cyclone of celebration carries them away; nevertheless, their episodes of reverie and silent pauses for meditation hinge upon the axis of that empty chair.

The inside world witnesses the outside world in perpetual impermanence. Buddha Hall is gone, the marble podium, gone. Where the tent once reigned is now open sky with sunlight and moonlight reaching the marble floor of what was once Buddha Hall. It now was part of a glen of polished marble called Buddha Grove, free of the forest canopy. Where disciples once sat before Osho, new generations of sannyasins join the old there to dance and meditate under the sun and stars. The new meeting hall is farther to the west incased in an air purified and great black pyramid that was under construction when last I was there in February-March of 2001. It is called Osho Auditorium…

Let's go back to the origin of Osho's Buddhafield.

Twenty-three years before the new millennium dawned, a bold Indian mystic with much more black hair in his white beard, sitting bare headed in a simple white robe woven of fine Egyptian cotton regularly sat upon another swiveling chair in the same spot on the podium every morning at 8 am. A smaller crowd of his disciples, dressed in various vibrant colors of the sunrise sat on a gray-stone tiled floor arranged around a grove of white cloth-covered poles suspending a far more rustic tent awning a mere 12 feet above their heads.

It is the morning of December 29, 1977 and at the time of this writing (19 November 2017) it is nearly 40 years earlier. Osho was addressed as Bhagwan Shree Rajneesh and he is giving the ninth discourse on Gautama Buddha's *Diamond Sutra*. On this morning he will share for the first time his vision of the transpersonal messiah—the Buddhafield.

"The word *Buddhafield* is of tremendous importance. You have to understand it, because that is what I am doing here—creating a Buddhafield. It is just to create a Buddhafield that we are moving away from the world, far away, so that a totally different kind of energy can be made available to you.

"*Buddhafield* means a situation where your sleeping Buddha can be awakened. *Buddhafield* means an energy-field where you can start growing, maturing, where your sleep can be broken, where you can be shocked to awareness; an electric field where you will not be able to fall asleep, where you will have to be awake, because shocks will be coming all the time.

"A *Buddhafield* is an energy field in which a Buddha matures beings, a pure land, an unworldly world, a paradise on earth, which offers ideal conditions for rapid spiritual growth. A *Buddhafield* is a matrix.

"The word 'matrix' comes from Latin. It means 'the womb.' From that word we get the words "matter," "mother," etcetera. The womb offers three things to a newly forming life: a source of possibility, a source of energy to explore that possibility, and a safe place within which that exploration can take place. That's what we are going to do. The new commune is going to be a great experiment in *Buddhahood*."

The audience listens, some staring in rapt attention at the man with the mirror eyes reflecting their faces, others sitting with eyes shut, enraptured by silence. All listen to the words; some even listen to the inner pauses between their master's slow and peacefully hypnotic cadences as he forms accented English words—sometimes with a soothing aspiration of "shhh"—from this trademark lisp.

The cuckoo in the gardens surrounding the hall calls out its rising glissandos of pure joy. A lonely train in the nearby station calls out a response, and Osho continues.

"Energies have to be made available to you: possibilities have to be made clear to you. You have to be made aware of your potential, and you have to be given a safe place from where you can work; a place where you are not distracted by the world, a place where you can go on without any disturbance from the crowd, a place where ordinary things, taboos, inhibitions, are put aside; where only one thing is significant—how to become a Buddha [an awakened one]; where everything else simply disappears from your mind— money and power and prestige; where all else becomes insignificant, when all else becomes exactly as it is—a shadow world—and you are no more lost in the apparent."

Twenty-three years before the new millennium a much smaller campus, called the Shree Rajneesh Ashram, surrounded Buddha Hall. The umbrella canopy of soothing tree shade had huge holes for the sun to beat down on the green buildings and bake the gravel thoroughfares. In 1977 the sun was hotter, the hair and beards were longer, the robes a louder orange and red and more folk-hippie in style. In 1977 this was the commune of the "Free-sex guru." A place of padded rooms where people wearing nothing more than sweat could take part in encounter groups, rebirthing sessions, and Tantric sex. This was the commune of the Rajneeshees of the Neo-Sannyas movement.

Osho had created a community of orange-robed men (and women) that rubbed traditional and patriarchal Indian ideas of the renunciate discipline of sannyas the wrong way. These new sannyasins didn't renounce life, they renounced non-acceptance of life. They forswore traditional religious dogmas that divided heaven from the world, making one sacred, the other profane. They sought to experiment with Osho's hypothesis that an integrated human being is part earthy Zorba the Greek and part otherworldly Gautama the *Buddha*. Osho called this synthesis "Zorba the Buddha."

The Orange People, as the press called them, experimented with the hypothesis that society programs inhibitions into us to retard our spiritual and material growth. To the Rajneeshees of that day, understanding your sexual energy was the key. Dive into it willingly and you might understand the root of life and unlock yourself from the inhibitions that stifle your life force.

Twenty-three years before the new millennium, when Osho introduced the concept of a new commune creating the force field of a collective Buddhahood, the climate of the ashram was essentially neo-Tantric—a revision of the ancient South Asian sect of conscious hedonists. In Tantra nothing is denied. You live with acceptance. You become a yes-sayer. Repress nothing—but Osho added one important proviso: be *aware*. Watch what you are doing, understand it. Use your witnessing consciousness to peel back all the layers of motivations that make you do everything you do each day, whether you are "doing" orgasm, misery, love, or hate—anything.

Osho asked his experimenting disciples not to believe him but to test his observations and insights. He invited them to experiment with his Ashram/Buddhafield's unique brand of active meditation techniques of self-observation tailored for the modern human being, who he claimed was too encumbered with thought and emotional repression to simply sit silently, doing nothing, like the disciples of Buddha 25 centuries earlier.

Those huddled close together on the cold gray stone floor on that December morning in 1977, listening to Osho expound the Buddhafield, were the vanguard of hundreds of thousands who would come to listen. Osho would give thousands of discourses over 20 years, covering everything under the sun: commentaries on all religions and their enlightened men and women masters, as well as observations on the sciences, history, Western philosophers, politics, and sociology—and always laced with thousands of jokes. The transcriptions of his recorded discourses would eventually fill 700 books."

If Osho was anything, he was progressive. He understood the mass media and their ability to record the utterances of future Christs and Buddhas. He understood that if Christ and Buddha had access to audiovisual technology it would have been much harder to make these extraordinarily ordinary and natural human beings into messiah myths. On videotape, the coming centuries would have seen them—warts and all—as ordinary people.

An audiotape or a home video showing what Jesus actually said during his Sermon on the Mount would have recorded *how* he said things. The subtleties of inflection, the pauses between words, would convey the nuances that no simple written record can capture. If his disciples had filmed Buddha's hundreds of discourses under the Bodhi tree, then for millennia to come future lovers of Buddha could have checked the accounts of his attendant and cousin-brother, Ananda, for any distortions.

Osho understood that new catalysts for the Buddhafield experiments of the Aquarian Age should use the objective evidence of audio and video recordings as one way to help root out self-proclaimed latter-day apostles who claim to have received "the truth." What luck would St. Paul have had when he broke ranks with Christ's brother James to proclaim Jesus to the Gentiles if videotapes existed showing Christ (or better, his true name, Yeshua) proclaiming his mission to be solely a Jewish spiritual revolution?

If technology had existed to record the founders of religions, the Vatican empires, Hindu hierarchies, and any other religious middlemen would have had to base their authority on something far more substantial and objective that the thin air of faith and the fading light of ancient memories.

Twenty-three years before the new millennium a tape machine at Osho's feet recorded one of his long and pregnant pauses before he continued speaking about what the Buddhafield would do to dispel illusion.

"Maya [illusion, sin] is to be caught up in the apparent. That is the greatest illusion in the world. The apparent holds such sway on our minds. A *Buddhafield* is a place where you are taken away from the apparent.

"In the silence of a commune, in the uninhibited, untabooed atmosphere of a commune, the master and the disciples can enact the drama totally. The ultimate is when the master can touch the feet of the disciple, when the master and disciples are lost into one reality."

In the year following this discourse, Reverend Jim Jones would lead his followers in a mass suicide. The world press tried to make comparisons between Jonestown and the Shree Rajneesh Ashram. Osho would explain that such a tragedy could never happen in his commune, because his people were there to celebrate life and renounce all that is life-negative. A false Buddhafield creates a Jonestown, or Hitler's Nazi utopia. The misery field can put on the mask of a Buddhafield while it magnifies the anger and fear. Paradoxically, a true master creating an authentic Buddhafield uses the collective love and meditation energy of its participants to forge equally unique individuals, not robots. It creates people to whom the master bows down in reverence—a new humanity.

"Now understand: if somebody says, 'I will create the Buddhafield,' and the emphasis is on 'I,' then the statement is false, because a person who has the 'I' still alive cannot create a Buddhafield. Only a person who has no 'I' within him can create a Buddhafield. In fact then to say he creates is not right; language is inadequate.

"The Sanskrit word for creation is far better. The Sanskrit word is 'nirpadayati.' It means many things. It can mean 'to create,' it can mean 'to accomplish,' it can mean 'to ripen,' it can mean 'to mature;' it can simply mean to trigger it into existence. That's exactly the meaning.

"A Buddha does not create, he triggers. Even to say he triggers is not good; in his presence things happen, in his presence things are triggered, processes start. Just his presence is a fire, a spark, and things start moving and one thing leads to another, and a great chain is created."

The disciples attending that discourse were already well aware of the miracle of so much creative activity buzzing around their lazy buddha bones. The ashram was a beehive of active meditation groups, therapy groups, Sufi and devotional dancing sessions, and a theater department. In addition there was all the hustle and bustle of the daily chores involved in feeding, clothing and cleaning for the thousands of guests and residents of the community—manning kitchens, running the medical center, clothing shops, and various other ashram industries.

Yet the man whose vision was responsible for all this activity did next to nothing all day. After rising in the morning he would move over to his chair and spend most of his waking hours sitting in blissful silence by the window next to a garden shaded by a great almond tree. It was as if his enlightenment had brought this "doing" to a complete stop. His only major effort of the day was to leave his room (which he called his "cave") and glide to the back seat of his chauffeur-driven Mercedes (and later a white Rolls-Royce), which carried him the few hundred yards to Buddha Hall and the waiting chair up on the podium.

He would come into the hall, lovingly greet his disciples with folded hands, sit, and discourse every morning for 90 minutes to two hours. Afterward he would rise, eyes glistening with a quiet tenderness, and fold his hands again to give his disciples a loving good-bye. The limousine carrying their guru would circuit the open walls of the tented hall, while the people within it followed its departure in hushed silence. The only commentary you could hear was the gravel against the tires, and the call of the cockerel as the car drove him back to his "cave."

In the evening, Osho would venture a few paces outside his room to a smaller pillared marble patio called Chuang Tzu Auditorium, named after the ancient Taoist master, and give sannyas initiation to disciples. In 1980-1981, and just prior to his personal initiations coming to an end, Osho gave what he called energy *darshans* at Chuang Tzu. He did nothing much more than sit in his chair and lay his long-fingered and finely sculpted hands on the brows of sannyasins.

The sessions would start with the candidates for the energy darshan being arranged around Osho sitting in his chair. At the right moment he would nod to the band, and guitars, sitars, flutes, and drums began stirring the air with ever more intense Sufi-zikur-style music. Around Osho and his candidates were a dozen red-robed female disciples dancing and moaning with abandon. This was a circle of the happiest, most energetic coven of witches one calm-eyed Indian warlock could ever settle himself among. The more relaxed he became, the more powerful was their dance, and the stronger the waves of music and energy coursing through Chuang Tzu Auditorium and echoing through the entire ashram compound. Just as the surge of music and dancing reached its climax, Osho would throw the *master* switch, putting out all the lights in the commune.

The unique experience of the energy darshans and high-energy blackouts was still a year or two away for the disciples listening to Osho's first Buddhafield discourse. In the peace of that December morning they heard him accurately foretell things to come, how thousands upon thousands more seekers would gather around him, and how their combined spiritual urgency, love, and uninhibited celebration would somehow deepen and empower Buddhahood's force field.

"That's how we have been going on. I simply sit in my room doing nothing, and seekers from all over the world have started pouring in. I don't even write a letter...just the presence. One comes, another comes, and the chain is created. Now the time has come when a Buddhafield is needed, a matrix is needed, because you don't know—thousands more are on the way. They have already moved, they are already thinking of coming."

The 1970s saw the Shree Rajneesh Ashram become the premier growth and therapy center in the world, but Osho found the semi-urban and wooded neighborhood of Koregaon Park too confining and nestled too close to the four million people living in the misery field of the overcrowded Indian city of Pune. There was constant friction from the neighbors and the city politicians. The Koregaon neighborhood of that day was too small to absorb the tens of thousands of Western disciples flooding its streets. They would overwhelm the limited apartment spaces and further crowd the riverside, establishing shantytowns of bamboo huts. The latter half of the 1970s saw his disciples comb India for properties far from population centers. Plans were made to build a new commune near the Rann of Kutch, a great marshland on the border of Pakistan in the western-most Indian State of Gujarat. Then the sannyasins considered another site near the Himalayan foothill resort of Shimla—but in both cases the politicians and influential Hindu fundamentalists sabotaged the projects.

In 1981, Osho at 50 was ailing and prematurely aging. He traveled to the US, allegedly to seek medical attention for a lower back condition. He began a three-year self-imposed public silence at a newly purchased 64,000-acre ranch in the high desert of eastern Oregon.

Between 1981 and 1985 a city of 2,500 permanent residents with the capacity to house another 25,000 temporary summer visitors would rise out of the Oregon desert in the largest Buddhafield of the twentieth century. An investment of $85 million, contributed from the communes and businesses of over 300,000 sannyasins worldwide, helped finance the construction of a city, a university, farming industries, and food and waste recycling systems. A highly successful ecological rehabilitation project was also launched, to heal the overgrazed ranchlands and degraded watershed. A new 88,000-square-foot greenhouse was later converted into a meeting hall with a seating capacity of over 20,000.

The new Buddha Hall, known as Rajneesh Mandir, became the main gathering place for thousands of disciples flying in from all parts of the world every July for mass satsangs with Osho during their international summer festivals. Where 1,500 and 2,000 disciples sat on a tile floor of gray stone listening to Osho introduce his Buddhafield vision in 1977, five years later a multitude of 25,000 people in shades of red sat or danced on all-American vinyl flooring before Osho on a podium, eyes closed, reclining in a chair under the vast roof of the Rajneesh Mandir.

I was one of the tens of thousands in that hall. One could feel the presence of an energy, a thrilling intensity in the atmosphere, whether 20,000 meditators sat like statues or twirled and swayed, singing and dancing before Osho's podium. Was Osho's Buddhafield experiment another excuse for brainwashing?

Yes!

A clean brain is much more fun to play with than one grimed with fossilized habits, fears, and hatreds. At the Oregon commune, surrounded by a red forest of thousands of individuals in meditation, it was easier to shake off all the dirt of the misery field. One lightens up in a Buddhafield. One smiles more, laughs more. Imagine living in a community where thousands of strangers accept you as you are, whether you are happy or crying, open or feeling closed and afraid. This is a place where it is easy to relax and be natural. You fall into synchronicity with its people, who in turn are emotionally and ecologically in harmony with their surroundings. You could leave your car or your front door unlocked, or forget your backpack on a downtown bench only to find it there the following morning. Here was a city where you could forget crime, where you had universal health care—spiritual as well as physical. You forgot the rat race. You found it easy to discard the heavy, life-energy-draining burden of day-to-day survival stifling your happiness, your creativity.

Osho foresaw such a place on that December morning in Pune in 1977 and the cumulative effect of many candles being lit by one flame.

"And the more people are there, the bigger the Buddhafield will be there, and the more powerful it will be. The possibility is that we can create one of the greatest and most powerful Buddhafields ever created in the world, because never before was there such search, because never before was man in such a crisis."

By the close of 1985, the experiment of the Oregon Buddhafield was over. Outside pressure from the surrounding misery field (known as the United States), along with the political intrigues of a small but powerful hierarchy that had emerged infecting the commune itself, resulted in Osho's arrest, and the disbanding of the commune.

I understand that around 1980, Osho may have publicly warned his disciples that if they chose to move the new commune to America, his vision of the future, of religiousness without religion, would see him arrested and murdered. I recall seeing that quote over 20 years ago. To verify that my memory is correct, I am currently tracking down Osho's exact words on this important and prescient statement. The prophecy, apocryphal or true, may have found its mark five years later thanks to a slow death by Thallium poisoning by the US government.

In early 1986, Osho, with less than four years left to live, returned to his room in the Pune Ashram and resumed his daily discourses, every evening at 7:00 pm. Where many sannyasins were bitter about the Oregon chapter, Osho saw his Buddhafield experiment there as a complete success, just a step along the way. It was the middle chapter of what some disciples close to him have told me was a three-step experiment.

I cannot say for sure the following theories are what Osho intended. They are my observations and those of other fellow travelers in his mystical caravanserai. They are based, for better *and* worse, upon the limits of what he playfully but earnestly called us, his buddhas (awakened ones) pretending not to be.

BUDDAFIELD ONE

The Shree Rajneesh Ashram of the 1970s was the earthly foundation of the experiment. It was a place where disciples refined their primal energies and sexuality and began clearing a lifetime of tensions, hatreds, and primal fears through catharsis. The energy was often raw. Foundations can be ugly, but I suppose a catalyst must base higher work upon a solid—if also hard and even gross—foundation.

BUDDAFIELD TWO

In the commune city in Oregon, work became the meditation. Step two also dealt with issues of power and its abuses. People learned they had the power to work miracles when they collaborated in harmony. The commune was a microcosm of the world, and for the most part its ordinary citizens experienced what the world could be like in the coming golden age if love and meditation were everyone's core commitment.

The world of the human communal family could work. It was creative, and ecologically and emotionally integrated. Wealth in all its dimensions—financial, spiritual, and emotional—can be abundant in a community that nourishes the Buddhahood aspirations of its individuals, no matter what corner of the world or what social or religious background they came from. Going beyond your limits was the revelation—even going beyond the limit of believing their second Buddhafield experiment could endure.

Much has been debated to this day inside and outside the community of disciples and devotees about what were the reasons and who was to blame for the fall of the Oregon Buddhafield experiment. I will say essentially this: old habits learned from life in the Misery Field eventually resurfaced to destroy its future. The citizens of the Oregon Buddhafield learned a harder lesson about the abuse of power when certain leaders of the ranch took advantage of Osho's public silence to twist his message of trust, send false messages in his name, and set themselves up as a little fascist regime.

When at last Osho broke his silence, he didn't confront the perpetrators like Moses coming down from Mt. Sinai lugging tablets. Over time the general tenor of his words at nightly discourses to the community at large did that for him. The talks expose how out of touch the growing totalitarianism of the leadership appeared when compared with Osho's vision of a free and individually responsible new humanity living in a global Buddhafield.

As stated before, you can only sustain negativity in a Buddhafield for so long. Finally the ringleader, Ma Anand Sheela and her followers, pulled up stakes and left town. Osho and the new administration invited the outside state and federal police into the commune to investigate the crimes committed against its citizens by the previous leadership. The crimes committed against people outside the commune by Sheela and her followers gave right-wing Christian elements in the Reagan administration the pretext to turn on Sheela's other victims. These were the people living "in" the Commune. The Reagan administration wanted to destroy the commune for their own religiously extreme reasons, and shut down Osho's second Buddhafield, the teaching of which they did not understand and therefore out of fear wanted to destroy.

Many disciples pulled by their own misunderstanding abandoned Osho and his experiments after the Oregon ranch era. To them Osho had falsely promised paradise. He was a false messiah, a charlatan. At the very least, he was not upholding their expectations—something even these disgruntled disciples have admitted is the only real promise their master regularly said he'd keep.

Those disciples who rejected these spiritual sour grapes and stayed for the next step in the Buddhafield experiment generally explained to me that Osho was constantly cleaning house in an effort to get rid of negative and selfish people—or those who took Osho, his communes and themselves too seriously, rather than sincerely.

A Buddhafield constantly needs to clear space for new experimenters willing to go deeper into the mystery of the Buddhafield journey. In other words, a Buddhafield is like a pond. People flow in and out, keeping it fresh. If people can't let the stale waters of their expectations constantly flow out of the pond, then they themselves stagnate, and the master provides them with reasons to flow out of the pond and seek their destiny elsewhere.

BUDDAFIELD THREE

Osho eventually returned to his Ashram in Pune in early 1987. After his deportation from the United States in November 1985, he embarked on a world tour to meet his scattered disciples in their own lands. US agents hounded his Lear jet wherever it went and succeeded in sabotaging his plans. Eventually he was either denied access to, or thrown out, of 21 countries.

Osho returned to India and for a time continued his discourses in an apartment in a northern suburb of Mumbai (Bombay). Eventually the controversies died down enough for him to return to his "cave" in the Pune Ashram. By this time both the Indian and American governments had somewhat relented in their efforts to deny visas to his disciples.

The third stage of the Buddhafield takes us to the present day. One might surmise that the physical death of Osho, in 1990, would test the survivability of his Buddhafield. With their leader gone, the disciples must live his vision, rather than listen to him talk about it.

Before he died, Osho appointed an inner circle of 21 disciples to manage the affairs of his communes. In the years following Osho's death crises have come and gone amongst the disciples about the direction of his vision. So far, it seems the momentum generated by meditation and the Buddhafield still works to soften disagreements between disciples and that inner circle.

The first month of the new millennium saw the ten-year anniversary of Osho's death. At the opening of a new century, the Pune ashram was now called the Osho International Commune and it continued to flourish. The Pune Ashram of old had exploded in growth. The 32-acre site then dominated Koregaon Park, and the commune offered visitors three dimensions of participation in the Buddhafield experiment. Meditations were offered throughout the day. There were nine faculties of the Osho Multiversity, including martial arts, creative arts, healing techniques, and esoteric sciences; or you could choose a Zen working meditation, where I suppose you could experience whistling and witnessing while you work in daily activities.

Whatever your pleasure, the religious atmosphere in the early decades of the new century at "Club-Meditation" (as the commune was playfully called by its managers) was light and carefree. Perhaps the most radical aspect of Osho's Buddhafield experiment is the contention that religion is fun, and that humor is a sacred prayer. Seriousness is a disease of the misery field—enlighten up!

Osho clarified this and other aspects arising from phase three of his Buddhafield after returning to Pune in 1987: "When so many people are relaxing into silences of their hearts, moving away from their minds, their past, their future, and are just remaining in the present, it creates a certain energy sphere, a certain vibe, a tidal wave that you cannot see. But if you are here, you will certainly be affected by the energy generated by so many people's silences... This is the purpose of the whole gathering of seekers of the mysteries of existence. Without making any effort to help, their very being becomes a magnetic pull. I call this field the buddhafield, the field of awakening." (*The Rebel*, 1987)

Initially, in the decade following Osho's corporeal departure, the numbers of new seekers at the Pune International Commune (currently as of November 2017 called the Osho International Meditation Resort), far exceeded the crowds of the 1970s. The Global Connections office at the Resort reported that the number of nations represented by visitors had jumped from 35 in 1990 to 110 countries by 1999. If such trends could continue, I thought Osho's movement would, over the coming decades, fulfill its founder's dream of spreading the presence of a Buddhafield across the world.

When Buddha peacefully left his body at the age of 84 his last words to his gathering of disciples were, "Be a light unto your Self."

Osho's last words to us were, "I leave you my dream."

These final statements of great masters contain the challenge and the responsibility of the disciples left behind, to be the light of the master that was his dream for us to attain. I have heard Osho say that when he is gone the responsibility of all those devoted to him becomes greater, to live in the light of the master, to be that light, which has always been *your light*. We have only forgotten.

The master had served as a remembrance of that light. His physical presence was an objective revelation that it is possible for every human being to be subjectively *This*.

I understand his dream to be living his light and being his light, which is my light, equally, eternally. Just remember each moment. Let go into *this, this, 10,000 times this moment*.

Upon *This* understanding, the management of the affairs of the community of sannyasins left behind, including their properties, retreats and meditation centers will find a harmonious evolution and expansion. Love springs from such a light and each member, whether they have responsibilities of running or visiting the estate of the master need to work and understand each other through the light of love. Both sides need to be equally response "able" through love and remain open and tolerant to each other. If negativity should arise, I heard Osho say the disciples should cathart negativity out in private and never bump "their stuff" on each other. Only come together to discuss a problem when the heat of anger is no more.

To live and be Osho. That is the question.

Different views of what that is will invariably arise, just as they did after Buddha Gautama's departure from the world. It is said that 24 hours after Buddha died his disciples split into at least 23 separate sects. It is only natural—or at least such is the case of those striving to be a light dispelling their own darkness—that conflicts and misunderstanding will arise. That all sides of a dispute on how to live and be Osho in their own lives might fall for the temptation, with all well meaning intentions, to believe they understand Osho better than other disciples. Perhaps only the few enlightened among his people might not be tempted.

Since Osho's physical departure in early 1990, there have surfaced some challenges, some travails of birth, going on for the *Sangha* (the spiritual community) without Osho physically present. They have intensified since the dawning of the new century and have been mainly centered on disagreements about how the Meditation Resort disseminates his books, his audio and videotape recorded discourses and what is the role of the main resort in relationship to other sannyasins and centers around the world.

The primary and longest lasting rift has developed because of legal battles over trademarking Osho's name which has seen other meditation retreats and resorts following their own understanding, independent of the Pune Resort's board of directors.

I am not here to judge for or against the merits of either side's stance but simply try to disseminate the consequential facts stemming from the rift. The Resort's right or wrong decision to ban longtime disciples of Osho from entering the "Club Meditation" Resort aside, the fact is, attendance at the Resort has declined in the second decade of the twenty-first century.

I have dear friends on both sides of this dispute; some of them are members of Osho's inner circle, a committee of 21 disciples to which he gave a few guidelines around nine months before he left his body. Not long after Osho departed his body, I had friends at the highest positions overseeing the Resort tell me a lot of details of what were Osho's dreams for the Resort. Many of these they miraculously managed to fund and construct, such as the pyramids, the Osho Teerth Park, the expansion of the Resort with wonderful recreation services, the Osho Guesthouse, a multistoried hotel for visitors next to the new "Buddha Hall," the striking black marbled pyramid known as Osho Auditorium. Many of the stunning buildings Osho dreamt about have been constructed and a most beautiful parkland now exists for citizens of Koregaon Park and Osho's meditators to enjoy. However, as I bear witness to hearing in detail Osho's vision of the resort, other dreams are left to be fulfilled, the most important of which is this: greater numbers of visitors coming from every corner of the world, far larger numbers than those during his lifetime, have yet to pass through the newly constructed Gateless Gate.

Osho's trust in his disciples is total and as a forecaster with some documented reputation of accuracy, I too foresee those far pavilions, the clock, and the multitudes that will come through the Gateless Gate happening. It can only be delayed. If it is not achieved by this generation of sannyasins who walked with him and sat with him, then I know it will be accomplished by future generations of sannyasins who discover how to live and be Osho without physically walking or sitting at his feet.

You can hear him explain how in the video *I Leave You My Dream* when his voice is heard over the beautiful scenes of disciples in the Pune resort celebrating his death and transfiguration: "The day I go, your responsibility becomes greater. To live. To live me, to become [pause] *me*. My leaving the body will be a challenge for you. That now that I have left one body, I can be in all of your bodies. And I am absolutely certain, utterly happy, that I have got the right people who are going to be my books, my temples, my synagogues. It all depends on you, because, who is going to spread me all over the world?" (*From the False to the Truth* [1985])

The video ends with Osho saying, "I am an incurable dreamer. No miracle ever happens unless you make it happen. I want this ashram to be the first synthesis between religiousness and scientific approach to life. This will fulfill my dream that the inner and the outer of man are not separate.

"When I'm saying this is going to happen, I am not saying it. I'm simply a vehicle to the Existence. I know perfectly well when it comes from my absolute Nothingness it is a message from Existence itself. It is going to happen. Nobody can prevent it. And this is the only hope for the New Man and the New Humanity." (*Om Mani Padme Hum* [1988])

I heard Osho in 1985 once say that the mainstream of humanity would understand his teaching a century hence. That would place full understanding and acceptance of Osho's dream of a new humanity fully flowering in the 2080s.

In the prophecy field, I am ever interested in reading the signs of how bridges to potential golden futures are step-by-step manufactured or evolve from the present day to that future time. I see one major stepping-stone on that bridge leading to the 2080s has already emerged. Awareness of Osho and his meditations has seen a significant Renaissance on social media and Internet that, in cyber space at least, has reconnected the global community of disciples and has greatly spread Osho's message and meditations across the world in a more significant exposure to the human race, and to the younger generations, than ever before.

For example, consider a simple experiment. Go to your YouTube browser and type in a search for, let's say, "Meditation Resort", the Osho Meditation Resort references fills the first page. Search for "Meditation Techniques" and Osho's video *Meditation Techniques for Contemporary People* is in the top ten. Most searches for "Osho" or Meditation will soon bring you to *OSHO.com*.

This devotee of Osho believes this jump to cyberspace marks a new evolution of the Buddhafield Experiment. Let's call it:

BUDDHAFIELD FOUR

I trust that the habits of controlling, reacting and the general seriousness casting a veil over the hearts of those on either side of this dispute will not stand in the way or censor the flowering of this new evolution of Osho's Buddhafield message overtaking cyberspace. The management at the resort are doing what they think is Osho's vision. Those against them presume their equally unenlightened understanding is better.

It must be remembered by those who love Osho who struggle with their expectations and conditionings of the mind, but love Him with every fiber of their being: listen to each other with an open heart and come together. Find a middle way to solve your challenges as a community.

Time is running out.

What Osho long foretold has begun. As predicted, and every year since we passed the year 2000 has seen a magnification of the old humanity moving into an auto-suicidal mode.

These times have arrived. A gathering of meditators and a spread of consciousness around the world has never been more needed than now.

The Buddhafield must grow stronger as the Misery Field reaches its self-destructive crystallization around the world— The Mind Plague. Those of us who bore witness to the birth of Osho's Buddhafield experiment all the way back on that December morning in 1977 or have joined it ever since need to be its joyous messengers by example. No missionary is needed. Simply be yourselves, loving, witnessing, and celebrating life each moment with laughter as our prayer. Seriousness and pontification need not be our *dis-ease.*

We are at the threshold of the 2020s. It will be the most dramatic decade of human reckoning. Does humanity destroy itself, or will it plant the seed of a Buddhafield that gives birth to a new humanity flowering in EVERY heart that beats?

It is now, more than ever before, that people will be ready to take a jump into religious experimentation because this *is* the ultimate time of human crisis. The coming 2020s will see unprecedented strains on traditional society. If Osho's Buddhafield can continue to grow, there's every possibility that millions of people seeking alternative answers will crowd the growing network of Buddhafield communities in the near future.

Twenty-three years before the new millennium dawned, a vision of such a future may have danced before Osho's eyes when in December 1977 he closed his first discourse on the Buddhafield with this declaration:

"We are at the threshold of something new that is going to happen to humanity. Either humanity will die and disappear, or we will take a jump, a leap, and a new being will be formed. We are exactly at the same point as millions of years ago when monkeys came down from the trees and humanity started and a new being was born. Again the moment is coming very close. It is a very dangerous moment, because there is every possibility... It was possible that the monkey may not have survived on the earth, he may have died on the earth, but a few monkeys took the risk. And they must have been thought of as fools by other monkeys—hmm?—who had always lived on the trees and were perfectly happy. They must have thought, 'these people are going mad, crazy. Why in the first place are you going to live on earth? Why create unnecessary trouble for yourselves? Our fathers and their fathers and their fathers have all lived on the trees.'

"Again the same situation is going to happen. Man has lived a long time the way he has lived. By the end of this [twentieth] century, a critical quantum leap is possible. Either man will die in the third world war or man will take the jump and will become a new man. Before that happens, a great Buddhafield is needed...where we can create that future."

Before he died, Osho predicted that he would be dissolved into his people, that wherever you met one of his sannyasins, or imbibed the tangible silence of one of his Buddhafield communities, there his presence would be, shining in the bright faces of his people, celebrating their passion for life, and meditating in their silences. By establishing a Buddhafield that shows no significant sign of diminishing because of his death, but evolving into new realms like cyberspace, Osho may be setting a new standard for all future gurus of the Aquarian Age. They may take his lead and dissolve any cult of messianic personality into the transpersonal phenomenon of their own versions of future Buddhafields.

The master in all of his actions is a means for remembrance. The future will gauge the success of masters of the Aquarian Age when their final gift, their physical departure from this earth, works to liberate the disciples from attachment to their bodies, and the danger of becoming just another distortion called "the Messiah" of another, spiritually dead, established religion, bereft of "religiousness."

If religiousness spreads all over the world the religions will fade away. It will be a tremendous blessing to humanity when man is simply man, neither Christian, nor Mohammedan, nor Hindu.

Religiousness is an individual affair. It is a message of love from you to the whole cosmos. Only then will there be a peace that passeth all misunderstanding.

Osho (1987)
The Greatest Challenge: The Golden Future

When will the Crazy Stop? The Great Paradox

The crises foreseen for the early to mid twenty-first century will be global. The only option for safety is to turn one's attention within to that still and silent point where a constant state of consciousness witnesses the storming and ever-changing world without fear or identification.

In the end, to save the world we must save ourselves. The forest, like the concept of humanity, is an abstraction. There is no forest, there are only individual trees. There is no humanity, there are only individual human beings. If enough people seek their individual enlightenment, and understand how they each contribute their individual portion of unconsciousness to the world's woes, then a great paradox can happen. If there are enough people who share this insight—if they turn their intelligence away from the forest, as it were, and train their full love, awareness, and understanding toward becoming individually healthy trees—then the whole forest called "humanity" will be saved.

"You are the world... Be alert not to contribute anything that makes the world a hell. And remember to contribute to the world something that makes it a paradise. This is the whole secret of a religious man. And if every individual starts doing it, there will be a revolution without any bloodshed." (Osho [1986] *Sermons in Stones*)

"You are the only hope! So don't keep your joy to yourself, spread it, make it available to anybody." (Osho [1985] *From the False to the True*)

"Truth not only saves you, it also saves others through you. Truth not only becomes freedom to you, it becomes a door of freedom for many others also. If you become a light, it is not only your life that will be lighted—if you become a light then you also become a light for millions; many can travel and reach their goal through you. If you become a light, you become a representative, you become a Christ.

"I don't want you to become Christians—that is useless, that is a lie. I want you to become Christs. And you can become Christs, because you have the same seed." (Osho [1974] *The Mystic Experience*)

Born Again Each Moment into *The New Man*

The cover of this book is a picture of me just a few weeks before my body's 25th birthday, enjoying an initiation into a "new birthday" of the spirit on 15 October 1980 in Pune, India. It was evening, 7:20 pm Indian Standard Time, and this second birth happened under the circular and pillared roof of the intimate, open-air, Chuang Tzu Auditorium. The man giving me my new life is Indian mystic and history's most unique, "spiritual rebel"—Osho.

You might wonder what was so "terrifying" about this "spiritual" man. Well, for one thing, he wasn't a serious man, but profoundly sincere. He clearly pointed out how all seriousness is a disease and the most serious cancer that had retarded the progress of human enlightenment were ALL the organized religions, large or small as enlightenment's profoundly unconscious gate keepers.

He taught life, love and laughter, celebration and meditation as the authentic truth of religion. He taught that when all the organized and spiritually corrupt religions faded away that would be the moment when humanity was free to simply be "religious." There will be a day when a maturing humanity will discard all the manmade personifications of an imaginary friend called "God." After that we will rediscover that our "Godliness" was our very nature and that as above, so below, Godliness is everywhere and everything because it is also "no-thing" at "ALL."

It is your nature, the nature of the Cosmos—you are THAT. Each of us, therefore, dwells in this very place of our body as buddhas (Awakened Ones) who have only forgotten our eternal birthright. Moreover, this very place, wherever your body resides right now, is a paradise of the here and now. You can glimpse this if you relax, watch and lift the veil of the programmed mind that has been placed in the way to help prevent you from seeing this hidden harmony. All you need to do is re-member, becoming one with this moment. Undivided. Letting go. Relaxing into the silence where the miraculous eternity resides ever inside, ever NOW.

Osho was humanity's number one rebel prophet as well. He foresaw the coming of "Homo Novus" the New Man and defined that new human "being-ness" in this way:

***

The most important need of humanity today is to be made aware that its past has betrayed it; that there is no point in continuing the past—it will be suicidal—that a new humanity is absolutely and urgently needed. And the new humanity will not be a society in the old sense, where individuals are only parts of it.

The new humanity will be a meeting of individuals, where individuals are the masters, and society is to serve them. It will have many different aspects to it. It will not have so many religions, it will have only a religious consciousness. It will not have a despot God as a creator, because that implies the slavery of man. It will have godliness as a quality of ultimate achievement—a quality of enlightenment. God will be spread all over—in everything, in every being.

The individual, for the first time, will not be programmed; he will be helped to be himself. He will not be given any ideals, any discipline, any certain pattern; he will be given only a tremendous love for freedom, so that he can sacrifice everything—even his own life—but he cannot sacrifice freedom. The new individual will not be repressive; he will be natural, with no inhibitions, expressive of everything that he has; just the way plants express themselves in different colors, in different fragrances, each individual will be doing the same.

The new individual will not have the false idea that all human beings are equal. They are not—they are unique, which is a far superior concept than equality. Although the new individuals will not be equal, they will have equal opportunity to grow into their potential, whatever it is.

There will be no marriage; love will be the only law. Children will be part of the commune, and only the commune will decide who is capable of being a mother and who is capable of being a father. It cannot be at random and accidental. And it will be according to the needs of the Earth.

The new humanity will have an ecology in which nature is not to be conquered, but lived and loved. We are part of it— how can we conquer it? It will not have races, no distinctions between nations, between colors, casts. It will not have any nations, and states; it will have only a functional world government.

The new man is an absolute necessity. The old is dead or is dying...cannot survive long. And if we cannot produce a new human being, then humanity will disappear from the Earth. (Osho [1986], *Beyond Psychology*)

It is hoping against hope—but I still hope that the danger of global death will be the shock which awakens humanity. If man survives after this [twentieth] century, it will be a new man and a new humanity. One thing is certain: Either man has to die or man has to change. I cannot think that man will choose to die. The longing for life is so great...just to think that the Earth has become dead—no trees, no humanity, no birds, no animals...it is such a great crisis. ...And if the third world war does not happen, that will mean a great change, a tidal

change in human consciousness. We will see a new man."
(Osho [1987], *The New Dawn*)

***

This message, this man, IS a spiritual rebel to those who
uphold and sustain the serious, dogmatic, enlightenment-
retarding, death-worshiping, nature-raping, old religions of an
Old Humanity mindset. They seem hell bent on destroying
themselves and the world. The old and fossilized mindsets of
the old religions ought to be terrified by this visionary. Just as
terrified as they were with spiritual rebels like Zarathustra,
Socrates, Buddha, Muhammad and Christ. Osho was murdered
and martyred like they were by the same political/religious
forces that would keep you serious, afraid, egocentric, and
being blind believers rather than experimenting *knowers*
achieving "knowing-ness" through direct experience of the
mystery of Existence.

If you find my writings unique and fresh, it is because I
have been a part of this being for 37 years and counting,
available to be born again and again, each moment ever since
he initiated me in this book cover's picture.

Since my second life was born in 1980, I side and move
with the spiritual rebels who only have true love, awareness,
and a rediscovered, innocent intelligence as their "weaponless-
weapons." Osho has taught me a religiousness that is alive and
bright with blissfulness.

Notice in that picture my eagerness to plunge into Him.
Notice his body, extending his hand to touch my forehead in
initiation. He is pure stillness. He is pure "Stop."

Can you see the profound emptiness? That isn't some
photographer's trick with lighting. Osho had a subtle glow
about him, emanating from him. Because I have known and

loved human beings like Osho, my words aren't hypothetical. I speak from the authority of first-hand experience.

I've been waiting for these times for 37 years and knew that when the world was approaching the 2020s, the coming decade would be a reckoning for our future. Humanity would either destroy itself or begin dropping its connection with the fossilized past, the mindset of the "Old" and "auto-suicidal" humanity, as Osho used to identify it. The time has now come to write far more about what your future can be and not so much about how you are currently destroying your future and the world.

From now on you will see me focus less on dire current events and more on the bigger, inner, picture of what is possible in each of us to bring the seed of a new humanity to flower.

It lives in the mud of the old and self-destructive humanity, the lotus of a golden future we can blossom.

I am a messenger, a "Sent Man" to all of you. I have good news to tell you. The new humanity is not someone else in the future. You are THAT humanity. You just have to start looking in, start questioning all that has been borrowed from others to create an ego-personality, under which you never were meant to be buried.

You don't have to wait more than a moment for his advent in the future. "You" are the New Man's future and "right now" is the only "eternity" called "The Present" that this new humanity has ever existed inside.

From now on my books and articles are going to slowly, slowly use the device of your interest in that future to point you to that present moment where you celebrate a happy birthday, this moment, each moment, inside *your* Golden Future.

The first step, the last step, is Meditation.

I call upon you all to answer this invitation to allow me to freely share with you information and leads to Osho's meditative techniques, tailored for the needs of the modern twenty-first century human being. All you have to do is contact me by copying this link into your browser:

http://www.hogueprophecy.com/new-contact-form/

Put in the email subject line just one word: **Meditation**.

I will then email you the links and information that can awaken the dormant seed of a new humanity that has ever waited inside you for this birth moment.

EPILOGUE
Childhood Ends
When Humanity *Golden* Ages

It may be that one of the greatest conspiracies against human beings has been the programming that convinces us that we as individuals cannot influence our collective destiny. But the need for human survival runs deeper than all the conditioning of the past.

The claim will be made that humanity never needed to grow up until faced with the unprecedented challenges of the twenty-first century. Up to the new millennium we could get along with a social structure that needed people to be functional mediocrities, and so ignored their potential for genius and Christlike consciousness.

It is foretold that traditional solutions will be discarded in the twenty-first century. The humanity of the future will celebrate innovation and find the courage to embrace the unknown. Armed with this new understanding forged in crisis, they will find their way out of the apocalypse of ecological disasters, fire, and war in the 2020s. They will awaken from the messianic pathology imposed upon them by a past-oriented society that could exist only by exploiting people's limitations, superstitions, and fears.

The coming stresses are predicted to destroy such a society. Humanity will therefore face the death of its past so that it can have a future.

By the end of the twenty-first century, religions as we have known them will fade away. We will see men and women of tomorrow, who have grown out of their childhood attachments to imaginary friends, gods, and sons of gods, and have matured into aware and response "able" individuals.

Our descendants will have discovered that no messiah outside of themselves is coming. Instead the Messiah descends to earth from his hiding place behind their worrying eyes. He walks the earth using their own feet. He speaks in a billion voices. He saves the world to abandon belief and trust in the unknown. Where they were once Christians, they now seek to be Christs. The Messiah is in actuality their collective awakening to their true natures.

At the dawn of the twenty-second century, humanity comes of age—the Golden Age.

THE END
(21 November 2017)

OTHER BOOKS BY JOHN HOGUE

BEYOND ALT-RIGHT, ALT-LEFT
A Community of Americans

World-renowned Futurist and Prophecy Scholar John Hogue didn't start noticing that telltale "clicking" of a government wiretap until 1997, when he was doing phone interviews on an international line patched into BBC Radio in the United Kingdom.

The gist of his forecast that got his phone clicking for the next six months was this: If future US Presidents and Congress continue to sustain and intensify a partisan deadlock between "Red" Republican and "Blue" Democrat legislators into the early decades of the twenty-first century, there will be a Balkanization of America, either caused by a bloody civil war or revolution, beginning by 2020.

Balkanization defines a country or region undergoing a violent process of fragmenting into smaller and often failing states at odds and often at war with each other.

The clock is running down. 2020 is only a few years away. According to what Hogue laid out in this new book, the United States is right on schedule. No moderation of the danger is in sight. Indeed, the momentum of political polarization of the United States dividing its people into Red and Blue Americas is now on steroids.

He cautions that before voices such as his are no longer wiretapped but potentially silenced or exiled, this concerned American wishes to share his forecasts and those of others American seers of the past that have not only anticipated these mounting dangers but can see the golden future possible beyond them. Hogue sets out in the book to first define the polarity clearly. If you are liberal or conservative, White

Supremacist or Antifa left-wing extreme, his compassionate hits and original take on things is fairly and evenly dispensed. He'll then take you on a journey beyond the hypnotics of the red and blue narrative bubbles that have suppress our basic, all-American sense of goodness, fairness, and tolerance for our neighbors.

In this book, Hogue writes: "A grass roots movement will emerge that uses the tools of the Internet to network what we share as common ground amongst a community of individuals. I call this revolution the Politics of the Fourth Way. It's not Democrat, Republican or even a third party. All parties are systems of collectivization of the individual. They are ever prone to corruption."

This short book will help identify the dangers inherent in extremist Left- or Right-leaning identity politics and offer ways to make the coming revolution and renewal of America creative and peaceful.

~~~~~~~

THE GREAT AMERICAN ECLIPSE
(21 August 2017)
Earthquake and Tsunami

Total solar eclipses seem to trigger seismic events upon the lands and seas their shadows touch. On 21 August 2017, the lower 48 states had a solar eclipse draw its mysterious darkness of 90 to 100 percent totality over four of some of America's most dangerous seismic and tsunami-generating quake zones. They are the Cascadia Subduction Zone in the Pacific Ocean along the Oregon, Washington and British Columbian Coasts; the dormant supervolcano in Yellowstone National Park; the New Madrid Fault Line in Missouri near the Mississippi River;

and finally, the earthquake-prone Charleston, South Carolina area along the Atlantic Coast.

If the pattern of seismic activity seen in the Great Eclipses of 1999 and 2009 is repeated in the Great American Eclipse of 2017, then either one or a series of potential major quakes of magnitude 6 to a megathrust of magnitude 9 could happen a week to three months after the eclipse. A second wave of seismic episodes of the same potential magnitude could follow 8 to 18 months after the eclipse. Less frequent but no less damaging episodes of quakes and tsunamis could take place as late as 2 to 5 years after the moon's shadow on 21 August 2017 had touched future epicenters inside these four seismically sensitive zones.

We would also see a spike in other natural disasters such as megafires and hurricanes. Indeed, the United States was slammed by an unprecedented series of massive hurricanes immediately after the eclipse took place. Four days after the eclipse, Category Four Hurricane Harvey inundated Southeastern Texas. Twenty-one days after the eclipse, Hurricane Irma slammed into the Florida Keyes a Category Four storm. A month after the eclipse Hurricane Maria made landfall on the US Territory of Puerto Rico as a Category Four knocking out the island's entire power grid and leaving behind unprecedented devastation. In early October, Norhern California suffered the deadliest and most destructive wildfires on record, burning down 7,500 houses, businesses and 16 Napa Valley wineries just around 48 days after the Great American Eclipse.

The eclipse is over but the coming months and upwards of five year of the aftermath as only begun.

World-renowned prophecy scholar and Nostradamus expert John Hogue will take us through a journey mixing seismic evidence with prophetic and astrological forecasts that will try to illuminate what will really happen, if anything, following the moon's shadow passing over America, from sea to shining sea.

The Great American Eclipse comes at a time of significant astrological portents that not only can bring a life-changing experience to President Donald Trump but also to 330 million Americans.

America is stuck and something has to give. Political fault lines in polarized Washington DC and fiat faults grinding out economic fantasy must rock, roll and rent.

Earthquakes can be a creative catalyst for unexpected uplifts of national attention that rethink, redefine and rebuild America for the better. This eclipse may mark the overshadowing of American hegemony over the world, yet John Hogue will share hopeful prophecies indicating that America's greatest and happiest days are ahead, once American is no longer burdened by being a superpower.

~~~~~~

JOHN HOGUE'S WORLDWIDE ASTROLOGICAL PREDICTIONS
For the Real New Year:
Spring 2017 to Spring 2018

John Hogue is taking the stars back to an "ancient" future. Tomorrow's astrologers will embrace what early astrologers and pagan civilizations understood: Spring is opening season of the natural New Year! Have your parties starting around the Vernal Equinox and continue to celebrate the transition of seasons all through April, Easter and up through May Day.

In the future, even Christmas will be moved to March when it will be discovered that Jesus Christ was born a "fish man" master, symbolized as a "fisher of souls," foreseen by ancient seers as the world teacher of the Piscean age. Two fish tied together represent Pisces. One represents the conscious, the other, the unconscious mind—both are engines of human predictability.

Hogue explains the papal origin of why New Year's Eve is celebrated in the dead of winter. He then takes us through the correct procession of changing seasons from birth (spring), peak life (summer), let go (autumn) and death's fallow peace (winter) exploring world events in the timeframe of seasons progressing in their corrected annual sequence. He will apply his 30 years experience of studying the astrology and medium work of Nostradamus to document highly accurate astrological forecasts—saddled to pure divination—that confounds astrologically dogmatic critics as it accurately illuminates.

This detailed and unique examination by a world-renowned astrologer and Nostradamus expert takes you through a detailed, day-by-day reading of coming world events. First he establishes what was astrologically "born" out of important worldwide elections from spring into summer of 2017 and then predicts the negative and positive consequences coming from August 2017 through June 2018.

Read one of the most detailed and comprehensive forecasts of the astrological significance of what happens during the Great American Eclipse in August 2017. More than this, Hogue prepares you for earthshaking changes that it will herald for America and the world in natural upheavals of the Earth, as well as political earthquakes, the renewed volatility of Wall Street, and the crises approaching for the fiat and global economy.

Hogue's future chronicles can be funny, shocking, even terrifying, but ever original and ultimately illuminating intense times lived in the death and rebirth of an age in ways only he can originally and accurately foresee.

TRUMP STRIKES SYRIA:
And North Korea?

President Donald J. Trump of the United States ordered an unexpected mass missile attack on Syria in April 2017, while he prepared a greater showdown against North Korea if, as he said, they don't "behave."

We have entered a new era of razor's-edged danger, rife with prophetic significance that world-renowned prophecy scholar, futurist and Nostradamus expert John Hogue can decipher and explain.

A rush to open confrontation, heedless of any actual investigation into who gassed who in Syria, is exacerbated by Trump's unprecedented game of matching aggressive bluff for bluff with the potentially unstable North Korean dictator, Kim Jong-Un, who may possess the capability to fire Intercontinental Ballistic Missiles tipped with nuclear weapons at the United States.

Nostradamus, clearly gave short and long countdowns to World War Three. One starts counting when a second cold war has started. That happened with the Ukrainian Civil War and a salvo of US sanctions and Russian counter-sanctions in late April 2014.

The short countdown is upon us. A worsening military crisis with Syria and North Korea could unleash a US-Russian nuclear exchange any time from now up through November 2017!

This book will take you into an alternative universe of facts over hearsay, skeptical inquiry over impulsive, uninformed and potentially history changing, and history "ending" international moves. It will investigate solid evidence beyond appearances and mainstream media manipulation to disclose just how potentially (and intentionally) uninformed Trump's decision may have been to strike Syria, and—perhaps any moment from now, attack North Korea—with earthshaking consequences for us all.

This future need not happen, and John Hogue will consult Nostradamus and other significant seers down through history that present for us alternative, positive choices we can make as we stand at this potent and potentially apocalyptic crossroad in time.

~~~~~~~

A NEW COLD WAR
The Prophecies of Nostradamus, Stormberger and Edgar Cayce

Prophets, such as Nostradamus, Stormberger, and others introduced in this new and topical book by world-renowned prophecy scholar John Hogue, accurately dated, detailed and forecast the coming of the First, the Second, and perhaps have anticipated a *Third* World War. They never foresaw the last cold war ending in Armageddon; yet, they do predict a new cold war between America and Russia "in our future" would merely be a short prelude to the threat of a civilization-ending nuclear war that no one saw coming. This book sounds a prophetic alarm while there's still time to stop the Third World War from happening. Explore these prophecies. Let them open your eyes wide with an awareness that can yet save humanity from walking, with eyes wide shut, into its greatest catastrophe.

THE ESSENTIAL HOPI PROPHECIES

The Hopi are Southwestern Native Americans dwelling in Pueblos of Oraibi. These are the oldest continuously inhabited settlements in North America dating back as far as 1100 C.E. Up until the mid-twentieth century, the Hopi kept a secret, an oral tradition of foreknowledge—signs presaging an end of an old and perhaps a beginning of a new world. The milestones listed are specific. For instance, they anticipated the coming of white people from the East laying down their iron roads with their iron horses. Later they would draw "cobwebs" of airplane contrails crisscrossing the skies. Then came the "Gourd of Ashes"—a metaphor describing the mushroom cloud in the shape of a round gourd stood on its long neck. The test firing of the atomic bomb near Hopi lands was taken as a sign to share the final Hopi Prophecies to people of all races. These herald the world's oncoming purification either by the fire of nuclear war and runaway global warming, or by a fire of a burning love and conscious concern for the Earth and each other.

Once again author and prophecy scholar John Hogue takes a large and involved prophetic subject and distills it down to its essentials for a quick and comprehensive read that includes the shared visions of many Native American nations about the coming of the Europeans to North America and the death and renewal of our world.

NOSTRADAMUS AND THE ANTICHRIST
Code Named Mabus

ANTICHRIST...

The name for the personification of evil. He's the Agent Smith shadow cast by every messianic Neo trying to save those in the Matrix of illusion. He's the opposite of Christ the "anointed one of God."

The great sixteenth-century physician and seer, Michel de Nostredame (1503–1566), better known by his Latinized nome-de-plume, Nostradamus, foresaw not one, but three Antichrists. Each would be responsible for taking humanity one step towards the world's complete destruction.

This is the hottest prophetic detective case discussed among an estimated 20 million Nostradamus fans around the world. All signs are that we are living in the days of the Third Antichrist. It is time to decode the enigma of Mabus—the third and final man of evil who stands in the way of Nostradamus' most cherished alternative destiny set for our future: a Millennium of Peace on Earth.

This thought provoking eBook will transport us through dark and prophetic shadows to uncloak the man who would be king of Armageddon. World renowned Nostradamus and prophecy expert John Hogue, invites you to use this book as a manual for future-sleuths interested in unlocking clues to a preventable mass murder of humanity. There are indications in the prophecies of Nostradamus that we have Free Will. We can forestall oncoming calamity. We can change the future by changing our actions today and expose the bloody hand of Mabus before his martyrdom causes Armageddon.

FRANCIS
And the Last Pope Prophecies of St. Malachy

In 1139 St. Malachy set out from Ireland on a harrowing pilgrimage to Rome, upon sighting the Eternal City he fell to the ground and began murmuring Latin verses, each signifying the future destiny of the popes. His words were suppressed for over three hundred years by the Roman Catholic Church, yet to this day 90 percent of the saint's prophecies have come true unfolding in chronological sequence in 111 Medieval Latin mottoes, and a final coda, that together hide clues identifying the succession of 112 Pontiffs up to Judgment Day.

Pope Francis is the "Last Pope."

John Hogue, noted Nostradamus and prophecy expert and author of the first major work on St. Malachy's prophecies "The Last Pope: The Decline and Fall of the Church of Rome" (1998), distills this fascinating subject down to the essentials in a quick, yet comprehensive, read focusing primarily on the last 36 pontiffs on the list. These are the men who would be Vicars of Christ foretold after St. Malachy's papal prophecies were rediscovered and published in the mid-1590s.

Up to that point all the preceding 76 mottoes had an unheard of 100 percent accuracy, leading Hogue to suggest these were not written by St. Malachy but recorded by someone from the 1590s hiding behind a saintly pseudonym. Hogue explains that all credibility for any list of fake prophecies plummets because forecasts published "after" the event are always perfect. Unlike the usual fraud, the 36 mottoes foretelling the fates of pontiffs after the mid-1590s remain remarkably accurate, up to 80-to-90 percent. They become clearer as the list counts down to the final pontiff.

EVERYTHING
YOU ALWAYS WANTED TO KNOW
ABOUT 666
But were Afraid to Ask

666 has fascinated, terrified and obsessed New Testament prophets, bible bashers, old-time religious end timers, and a pope-pourri of pontiffs for two thousand years. It's been the Voldemort of numbers—that which cannot be named in decent company—from the Holy Land all the way to Hollywood. Arnold Schwarzenegger on the eve of the millennium's turning got his glocks off, sick-six-sexy with the purported number of the Beast of Revelation in his film End of Days.

It's time to lighten up about this trio of sixes. They get in a lot of trouble and unfairly stand alone for the most demonic number in the world, even though they have company.

666 isn't the only number of the Beast out there. The oldest surviving fragment of St. John's Book of Revelation, found in Egypt in the 1990s, proves there's more than one number upping the Anti-Christ, applying the numerical values of Greek and Hebrew letters to spell out the name of the Beast in The Book of Revelation, Chapter 13—Friday the Thirteenth, Jason style.

The title of my book is both outright and an outrageous homage to that other sinful number we all think about, but are too afraid to ask on a date—sex.

David R. Reuben came up with a brilliant idea in 1969 to author an enlightening and entertaining book called Everything You Always Wanted to Know About Sex, but Were Afraid to Ask. Then Woody Allen immortalized it in the hilarious film by the same name released in 1972.

Now, I'm not trying to pull Woody away from blowing his clarinet with the boys at the Cafe Carlyle on Mondays to make us a Sunday School feature film. All seriousness aside, I do think it's high, holy time all of us with an interest in comparative prophecy study "get down," grin, and bare all the things we're afraid to ask about 666.

So reach out and touch some Kindle Reader and enjoy a quickie—I mean, read this quick and informative, funny eBook all about those devil-made-me-do-it-digits.

PREDICTIONS OF THE LAST BLOOD MOON

The fourth and final blood-colored eclipse of the moon took place at the end of September 2015. It's the last portent of the current and rare lunar tetrad that's supposed to launch what some Christian theologians, such as John Hagee, promote as the beginning of the End of Days, unto Judgment Day. Is there more than mere religiously hyped "sky is falling" chicken-feathered hysteria fanning up a tall tale here? Could the last appearance of a reddened moon mark into motion something that even its chief proponents have overlooked?

We've all been here before with authors creating book franchises anticipating, and pimping, the end the world. There was the Millennium (computer) Bug of 1999, and Doomsday scheduled for the Year 2000. Then came the Mayan Calendar craze of 2012.

In this new attempt to restore clarity to an over-popularized prophetic tradition, Hogue explains that Blood Moon Prophecy, just like the Mayan Calendar 2012 predictions, has significant elements of revelation worth exploring if only someone could clean off all the hype, and push the pause button on Christian fundamentalist expectations.

Unique to this book is Hogue's introduction of astrological and non-Christian parallel visions that often prefigure clearer and more accurately timed signs of history-altering changes forewarned.

Go moon gazing with a bestselling author who exposed the "new age sewage" beclouding 2012 prophecies in this breathtaking as well as concise and sometimes satirical investigation of those who play "Chicken" a "Little" too broadly with Christian Bible prophecy. The sky may not be falling where and when they think it

NOSTRADAMUS: THE WAR WITH IRAN
Islamic Prophecies of the Apocalypse

Never has Nostradamus "come into the clear" like this, naming names, accurately dating events and places outright about a war in the Persian Gulf between America and Israel against Iran. Ships will be "melted and sunk by the Trident"! Is he speaking of US trident nuclear missiles, or, the mysterious trident hidden in the Iranian flag? This war is dated to happen after an interlude of peace negotiations in 2014 lead to the worst region-wide conflict the Middle East has ever seen. Armageddon, perhaps? That depends on accessing Nostradamus' alternative future hidden in prophecies written over 450 years ago. Peace is possible, dated for the last dark hour before a war that will change the live of every human being.

NOSTRADAMUS
A Life and Myth

John Hogue published the first full-bodied biography of one of the most famous and controversial historical figures of the last millennium. He traces the life and legacy of the French prophet in fascinating and insightful detail, revealing much little known and original material never before published in English.

~~~~~~

NOSTRADAMUS
The End of End Times

Read John Hogue's last—and often satirical—word on Mayan doomsday or "bloomsday" and first word on the many other significant and ongoing reboots of prophetic time cycles that a fawning paparazzi obsession with the Mayan Calendar had overlooked and neglected while they are still transforming human destiny.

~~~~~~

THE ESSENTIAL NOSTRADAMUS

Nostradamus, the 16th-century physician and prophetic giant, has a lot to say about the 21st century and beyond. The man who hundreds of times accurately foresaw Napoleon, Hitler, the world wars, and the American, French and Russian revolutions and men walking on the moon, did not lay down his pen after seeing the events leading up to the year 2012. His history of the future continues for at least another 1,785 years!

This is a rare little book giving you the low-down on a big subject: Nostradamus, the man, his magical practices and a brief but comprehensive overview of his greatest past, present, near future and distant future prophecies. It presents for your attention a quick exploration of those prophecies that will directly affect you sooner than you can imagine.

THE ESSENTIAL NOSTRADAMUS WILL TELL YOU ABOUT:

—Nostradamus' astonishing prophecies of the last four centuries.

—His mysterious double life, lived in intolerant times.

—The secret practices that opened his eyes to see the future.

—Nostradamus warned us of a "King of Terror" descending from the skies after July 1999. See who he or "it" was when "1999" hides the real date "9.11.1."

—Prophecies over four centuries old that described in clear detail the flaming impact of hijacked jets into New York's World Trade Center towers on 11 September, 2001, the US invasion and occupation of Iraq and the rise of the "black terror" called ISIS.

—There will be a 27-year war of a terrorist leader called "Mabus" the "Third Antichrist."

—A second cold war threatens a Third World War if it goes prophetically unrecognized.

—Visions of a distant future of extraterrestrial first contact and the human colonization of the stars.

—Nostradamus' visions foresee a 21st century either afflicted by planetary ecological catastrophe or blessed by a millennium of peace. The choice is ours.

TRUMP FOR PRESIDENT
Astrological Predictions

Take Donald Trump seriously. He's in the race all the way to become president of the United States. The bombast, the buttons he pushes to get people in a distracted nation talking about women's equality and illegal immigration are primed and fired for affect. We're talking about "The Donald" here, at a time in US history when a New York City real estate developer-cum-television celebrity and multi-billionaire business tycoon has saved away decades of collateral attention for his political close-up. He's carefully stockpiled the silver bars of bad press with the gold bars of good. He's let you have a tantalizing glimpse, year after year, on NBC's *The Apprentice* and *Celebrity Apprentice*, of just how smooth an operator a real chief executive can be. We've grown familiar with his style, his larger-than-life ways all witnessed by a crowning shock of bleached-to-cherry blond hair.

Let me be frank with you, he has carefully collected a fortune of leverage made of another currency more subtle than mere money—the currency of notoriety and your familiarity. A sustained attraction for decades fashioned out of love or hate of Trump, works like a carrying fund payment on a property investment. It's time to spend it.

Donald John Trump approaches completing his 70th year on this Earth playing the Game of Life, gaming it well, doing what he loves, and enjoying himself terrifically. A good deal maker and investor has good timing. It's time to cash in. It's the right moment to raise the stakes in his game, thinking bigger than he's ever dreamed before.

Here he comes, and let me tell you, he's primed and ready to negotiate his biggest, most fantastic, most challenging, most stupendous deal yet: convince a majority of the American people to vote for Trump as their next president.

The stars clearly indicate that the subject of this book can take a punch if criticism is fair. Therefore, internationally acclaimed astrologer and prophecy expert, John Hogue, will pull no punches or deny any positive potentials in this unique astrological study of a genius promoter who may be the next president of the United States.

Love him or hate him, people of all opinions pro or con about Donald Trump will find something captivating, surprising and altogether illuminating in this thoroughly entertaining astrological examination.

PREDICTIONS 2015-2016

John Hogue, a world renowned authority on Nostradamus and prophetic traditions, will reveal the potential, history-changing events coming in the second half of 2015 as this year may be the last chance to begin reforming monetary, economic, and political systems. Otherwise, time begins running out to avoid a disastrous future that might ultimately entail a threat of human extinction from planetary climate change. Hogue will take us further, into the year 2016, and how it could become Year One of a 20-year period of "The Great Unraveling" as foreseen by Nostradamus.

Let that not dishearten you, cautions Hogue. In his most epic examination yet of worldwide prophetic trends, Hogue presents in breathtaking detail a thought-provoking encounter with tomorrow's many potentials, where even the scariest future collapse of old systems of order and centralization can also be cause for the rise of new people movements and positive socio-economic and political revolutions. These and other unexpected reversals of fate and fortune are waiting that may nullify many clear and present threats to human survival and individual freedom that seem set against our pursuit of a happier, and golden, future.

Sample Chapters

An excerpt from
BEYOND ALT-RIGHT, ALT-LEFT
A Community of Americans

CHAPTER TWO:
The Alt-Left: A Spitting Image of the Alt-Right
Spilling Statues in Charlottesville

*There are periods in the life of humanity, which generally
coincide with the beginning of the fall of cultures and
civilizations, when the masses irretrievably lose their reason
and begin to destroy everything that has been created by
centuries and millenniums of culture.*

G.I. Gurdjieff (c.1916), *Meetings with the Miraculous*

A loving reminder: I say the following words with a peaceful
and compassionate heart. They are meant to help you. The skin
peeling of identity I am about to perform is necessary and
loving. If you read anything other than a state of even-
witnessing and quiet in my naturally descriptive and strong
words, then you are projecting your own suppressed emotional
issues upon them. Please remember that when reading the
following article addressed to those in the world who would
tear down statues and erase history in moments when these
words might trigger something inside you and make further
reading difficult.

127

Read on.

And if you see your anger rising, be a mere witness of it rising. It actually isn't "yours." Just watch thoughts, reactions and emotions, without being for or against them and over time you'll see them disappear as if you are a dreamer awakening from a long sleep.

What follows is a reality beyond wonderful.

Erasing history is not "learning" from history.

And yet, such acts of vandalism, whether by a government or an uninformed, hysterical mob mindset, are a common act at the end of great ages. A collective madness, fueled by a binary (0-1, black and white), intolerant and mediocre understanding of history fires the belly passions of the vacuous brained. Human beings become human "things" when they attempt to dispose of "things" that symbolize points of historical contention.

These "things" were once your neighbors, or your ancestors, represented in images and statues of the historically remembered dead. The historical literacy of those who would topple them seems to be as deep as the thin stain of pigeon poop splattering the statues. The intellectually challenged fixating on only one act of all-to-human error would topple symbols and overthrow the entire life and works of historical figures that helped our nation. All the good they have done is violently forgotten when mob-madness marches in the streets of Charlottesville, Virginia, on 11-12 August 2017.

It takes two to rumble. Left-wingers organized with their weapons of riot spoiling for a fight with right-wingers. The latter legally assembled in Charlottesville, a majority of which wished to peacefully assemble to protest the pulling down of Confederate statues of Robert E. Lee. No matter. Left-leaning ruffians sought out a willing minority of right-wing thugs in their ranks, equally armed, spoiling for a most unpeaceful assembly.

You young men and women on an anti-fascist crusade with sharpened fascist weapons in hand think statue crashing will clean the slate for righteousness by taking down General Robert E. Lee, just because you think he represents "only" a symbol of those who upheld slavery in the Confederacy.

Hold on a moment. Before you brain some neo-Nazi. Just how much do you know about the life and deeds of Robert E. Lee? Do you comprehend how citizens of America in those days felt about their states? That a man could defend his state from violent invasion as his reason and not in defense of slavery?

How many of you neo-Nazi baiters know that President Lincoln had sought out Virginian Robert E. Lee, the American Army's most gifted and respected officer, to lead Union forces to break the Confederate rebellion?

No memory spawns no virtue.

Be a force of mindless reaction. Hit that white guy with the Confederate flag while he's down, sprawled on the ground with your riot stick as photos of the Charlottesville riots show, even if the mainstream media fixated on the White Supremacists marching and Nazi saluting with Swastikas and Confederate Stars and Bars flags.

Tear down a statue of a Confederate soldier from its podium and spit on it like a barbarian from the Dark Ages or an Islamic State terrorist raiding an Iraqi museum to destroy statues of ancient Mesopotamian cultures.

Blithely have no clue how existentially torn Robert E. Lee was, a great and thoughtful man, when Virginia joined the Confederacy. Lee rejected Lincoln's offer and joined the Confederacy not to uphold slavery but to defend his countrymen from invasion. Only a rampaging hooligan cannot know what country and people Lee was defending. Who wants to bother their pea-brained mind with the many shades of "gray" that brought good men on both sides to join the blue and gray armies on the battlefield of the American Civil War? Few of you hooligans give a hoot that many men of the South could not bring themselves to fight and kill their own people, their sons and brothers, their fathers.

You cannot rightly judge the past if you don't understand how people of the past thought and felt. Back in those days, your state was first your country, gathered in a union of other sovereign states. Lee could not bring himself to fight and kill his own kin, his own people, the Virginians. Therefore he could not lead the Union Army to quell the rebellion and he made the hard and terrible choice to defend his people.

Be compassionately advised, I am not defending the worldview of White Supremacists or the Confederacy. The Confederacy's way of life was based on the social cancer of slavery and it took a civil war to cut that tumor out of America and so far, not with complete remission. In the next three chapters you can read a series of articles I published in the hot and racially charged days of July 2015 that angered as many of my white racist readers as this article is upsetting my leftist-supremacist readers right now.

Perhaps it is impossible to reach my white readers harboring racist misunderstanding. I'll keep trying because I love them as much as I love my liberally unconscious friends. For today, I will entertain the possibility that there's the slightest chance that I can reach those of you who identify yourselves as being "liberal" or "progressive" by illuminating just how "liberal" and "progressive" you really are, or are not. Then maybe you can love your enemies and have compassion for them.

When I see you behaving just like the people you hate, I see you becoming that which you hate. That's why I'm lovingly hitting you liberally-identified readers harder today. In a way, spouting liberal ideas but acting like a thug and a vandal of history makes you one thing the White Supremacists and American Nazis aren't, a hypocrite. We know where the racists stand. They show their faces openly at Charlottesville while the most violent liberals who clashed with them hid their faces like cowards, shrouded like ISIS jihadists do in black hoods—thug like.

An excerpt from
FRANCIS:
And the Last Pope Prophecies of St. Malachy

CHAPTER NINE
"Tribulation Futures, Past" from

Pope Francis is *Petrus Romanus* if St. Malachy's break with describing each pope unto the tribulation with a short Latin motto means he has come to the end of his list.

There is a chance that Malachy or the mystery composer of these prophecies sees Benedict's apostasy as a break in the proper flow of pontifical succession. That could mean the prophecy cuts to the chase, as it were, and jumps a few pontiffs and false popes ahead to the days of the last Pope "Peter".

Then again, Pope Francis embraced the name of a holy saint that includes "Peter" in his full birth name.

St. Francis of Assisi's Christian name was Francesco di *Pietro* di Bernardone. Thus, Peter of Rome can be Pope Francis because St. Francis was also called "Peter".

Other significant omens arise not directly related to St. Malachy that point to Pope Francis as a channel for the grace and mysterious patronage of St. Francis in his pontificate: the lightning striking St Peter's Basilica a few hours after Benedict XVI announced his resignation on 11 February 2013. Another great thunderstorm hit on the afternoon of 12 March. The sky opened with hailstones and a downpour the exact moment the conclave gathered behind the locked door of the Sistine Chapel and began the election process for a new pope.

Then the omen of the seagull.

It chose to perch on the stovepipe on the Sistine Chapel roof in the late afternoon of the second day of the conclave. It alighted there, after four votes had seen the stovepipe vomit black smoke indicating that no vote had yet reached the magic number 77 (two-thirds plus one) needed to elect a pope.

While the bird rested there for fully an hour, down the pipe and into the Sistine Chapel below its webbed feet sat Cardinal Jorge Bergoglio considering the unthinkable, being comforted by his friend, the 78-year old Brazilian Cardinal Hummes. With each ballot the tally increased under his announced name, hinting that by the fifth ballot held that evening, Cardinal Jorge looked certain to be picked the next pontiff.

Philip Pullella and Catherine Hornby, in their Reuters article *Pope Francis wants the Church to be Poor and be for the Poor* recorded the confessions of Pope Francis about the conclave in his first international press conference on Saturday 16 February:

[Pope Francis] recalled how on Wednesday night, as he was receiving more and more votes in the conclave, the cardinal sitting next to him, Claudio Hummes, comforted him 'as the situation became dangerous'.

After the voting reached the two-thirds majority that elected him, applause broke out. Hummes...then hugged and kissed him and told him 'Don't forget the poor', the pope recounted, often gesturing with his hands.

'That word entered here,' [Francis] added, pointing to his head.

While the formal voting continued, the pope recalled: 'I thought of wars.... and Francis (of Assisi) is the man of peace, and that is how the name entered my heart, Francis of Assisi, for me he is the man of poverty, the man of peace, the man who loves and protects others.'

Above his head, on the stovepipe's terminus, the bird, perhaps a sign from St. Francis himself, flew off at dusk. Not long afterwards, the white smoke was seen by the world.

Habemus Papam! (We have a Pope.)

Statues of St. Francis, known to be a great lover and protector of animals and nature, often depict him with a white bird on his shoulder or a bird tenderly nestled in his hand. This patron saint of Italy was also made the patron saint of ecology by John Paul II in 1979. With that in mind, the great storms upon Benedict's resignation and those pummeling the conclave could be portents of climate change overshadowing the new pope's reign.

It so happens that 2013 was the first year of a string of intensifying and significantly powerful El Niño natural disasters. The rash of violent weather that year prompted the first serious discussion by the world mainstream media that had already been ongoing amongst climate scientists who believed the intensifying *El Niño* phenomenon warming the waters of the Eastern South Pacific Ocean off the coast of Peru was evidence that greenhouse gases spewed by industrialization could cause a planet-wide *global warming*. This *Climate Change* could ultimately threaten the future of human civilization.

With these omens in my mind, I made the following prediction on 18 March 2013 defining the chief mission of Francis during his pontificate:

This new pope will take on the challenge of global warming as he has taken on the name of the Patron Saint of Ecology i.e. the defender and lover of the balance of nature in sky, air and sea, and the protector of its animals. So many species of plant and animal are now under threat of a mass extinction in the coming 100 years that the loss of innocent animal species might rival the great Cretaceous die-off of 65 million years ago when the age of dinosaurs ended in a cosmic and catastrophic natural disaster.

Mark you well, reader, the violent weather that struck St. Peter's dome when a pope resigned and struck it again with great hail and deluges the moment a conclave to elect his successor convened. That may have been the spirit of Ecology, the spirit of St. Francis giving omen to the church and Francis its new pope that the world's natural balance is upset and threatened.

Pope Francis Revealed in Catholic Prophecy
(HogueProphecy Bulletin, 18 March 2015)

"Right now, we don't have a very good relation with creation," reflected Pope Francis in his first press conference. He indicated how he would begin changing that, by following in the footsteps of revitalization and reform of St. Francis of Assisi. This pope, elected on the 13th of March at 8:13 pm, the first non-European pope in 1,300 years, will walk in the footsteps of the 13th-century saint so beloved by environmentalists because he loved, protected and tenderly preached to birds and animals.

At the end of the press conference, Pope Francis switched from Italian and spoke in Spanish. Smiling and tenderly he said, "I told you I would willingly give you a blessing. Since many of you do not belong to the Catholic Church and others are non-believers, from the bottom of my heart I give this silent blessing to each and every one of you, respecting the conscience of each one of you but knowing that each one of you is a child of God. May God bless all of you."

An excerpt from
NOSTRADAMUS: A LIFE AND MYTH

INTRODUCTION
"Tribulation Futures, Past" from

The 16th-century French doctor Michel de Nostradamus, and his obscure yet hypnotic prophecies, have cast their spell on the world over the last four-and-a-half centuries. He has become a wellspring for wisdom and waggishness for a broad range of diverse historical figures and colorful characters. He is a brunt of jokes by Jay Leno of NBC's *Tonight Show* and was the theatrical device of a cigar-waving Orson Welles, giving one of his better melodramatic performances as the host in a documentary, uttering facts, fables, and smoke rings as captivating and cloudy as Nostradamus' own writings. Nostradamus has been the inspiration for something as benign and silly as the Nostra Doormouse of holiday cards, while others exploited his prophecies for deadlier purposes. Josef Goebbels used the prophecies of Nostradamus as a Nazi propaganda weapon during World War II, while Britain's legendary prime minister Winston Churchill retaliated with his own platoon of interpreters, until even Louis B. Mayer, the movie mogul of MGM Studios, put Nostradamus on the silver screen in his film shorts to boost American morale.

Today, many dismiss Nostradamus as a freak of urban legends and reject his interpreters and avid students as victims of another reconstituted alluvium of New Age sewage. Nonetheless, he has had (and still has) millions of admirers and defenders. Some of them were kings and queens of France, including such rulers as Henry IV, Louis XIII, Louis XIV, and Emperor Napoleon's wife—the Empress Josephine. Respected literary giants such as Victor Hugo have tried to decipher him. World leaders have invoked his name to change destiny.

Nostradamus and his prophecies just won't go away. At the moment when it seems as if the tangle of biographical fact and myth about the man and the chaos of his cryptic prophecies should drive one away, lightning bolts of what appear to be prescient genius cut through his nebulous narrative of tomorrow.

Was Nostradamus a fraud or a true prophetic savant?

One thing is certain: It is safe to say that the man who launched the Nostradamian phenomenon has made good on at least one of his 1,500 or more predictions—that greater and lingering fame would come after his death. Indeed, after his passing in 1566, his "afterlife" has made his name far more famous and enduring than when he was alive. It cannot be denied, even by his greatest debunkers, that Nostradamus is one of the best-known historical figures of the past millennium.

When we, and the controversy of Nostradamus, entered a new millennium, many interpreters and dilettantes of Nostradamus mistakenly believed his prophecies foretold the end of the world—a strangely popular but patently unqualified myth, since Nostradamus had dated the end of the world 1,797 years ahead in the year 3797. Nevertheless, a peaceful turning of New Year's Day 2000 exposed Nostradamus in the minds of many believers and skeptics as a prophetic failure and charlatan. Then on 11 September 2001, the debate about this man and myth came back before global scrutiny. No sooner had the twin towers of the World Trade Center collapsed into billowing, apocalyptic clouds of debris, than Reuters News Agency broadcast across the planet a prophecy attributed to Nostradamus about "hollow mountains" falling in the "City of York." The lines of the purported prophecy—much like what we know about the man Nostradamus—were a blend of myth and fact. Fake lines like "the city of York" drew people in, yet these were sewn together with stolen lines of two actual Nostradamus prophecies—the same prophecies that for decades many interpreters, including this author, believed forecast a future nuclear or terrorist attack on New York's lower Manhattan financial district.

A prophetic hoax about an attack on the "City of York" rode on the back of these real quatrain (four-line) prophecies about what many believe is an attack on New York:

At forty-five degrees latitude, the sky will burn,
Fire approaches the great new city.
Immediately a huge, scattered flame leaps up,
When they want verification from the Normans **[the French].**

Garden of the world near the new city,
In the path of the hollow mountains:
It will be seized and plunged into a boiling cauldron,
Drinking by force the waters poisoned by sulfur.

(Quatrain 97, Century 6 and Quatrain 49, Century 10, *THE PROPHECIES OF M. MICHEL DE NOSTRADAMUS.*)[1]

When you have two prescient-sounding yet general provocations that include images like "fire approaching" a "new city" at "forty-five degrees latitude" in the "path" of "hollow mountains" near a "garden of the word," the hackles can rise—especially if you apply present-day facts to conveniently join together the dots of a 450-year-old prophetic rant to see what you want to see. Does one brush it all off as a coincidence that the city of "new" York is near latitude 45 degrees, or that the first Boeing 757 hijacked by terrorists cut into the North Tower of the World Trade Center in "a huge, scattered flame" at a 45-degree angle? Is it just the law of chance fooling a prophetically sympathetic mind when the second hijacked airliner passed over New Jersey (also known as the "Garden" state) and swerved at high speed toward the South Tower of the "world" Trade center building exactly over the "Path" subway tunnel before slamming into the second man-made peak of "hollow mountains"? And when Nostradamus describes his vision of "hollow mountains" being "seized and plunged" into a "boiling cauldron," are we conned yet again by a new generation of sycophants tagging events of their time on to cryptic ravings; or, is it more than a coincidence that each tower as it fell looked as if it were seized by the hand of an invisible force and plunged into the boiling cauldron of its own debris cloud? Are the "Normans" some retroactive allusion to the people of Normandy, or is this, as Nostradamian scholars believe, a code name for the French, whose intelligence agents on 10 September were indeed frantically warning their opposites in Washington D.C. that a terrorist attack on America was imminent?

Do we have a 16th-century charlatan catching us in our projections when the multiple meanings of Renaissance French can satisfy what we want to see? The word Nostradamus uses for "cauldron" is *cuue* (spelled *cuve* in Modern French). It can mean a number of things beyond "cauldron" such as "tank" or "tub." Is the skeptic right when he brushes off any application of this word to the fall of the twin towers? Is the skeptic right to suggest waggishly that we might as well say Nostradamus is predicting some future disaster in a jacuzzi; or, is it not a little disturbing to one's flippant reason to discover that the World Trade Center was built on a huge, rectangular cement box of watertight floor and walls known as "the tub"?

Welcome to the debate.

It could be said that Nostradamus the man planted the seed of Nostradamus the Myth in April of 1554 (on Friday the Thirteenth, no less) when it is believed his secretary began

140

transcribing his bizarre history of the future.The Myth was born 12 years later, in 1566, when family and friends lay his lifeless body behind the wall of his favorite chapel outside of town.

Ever since that day, Nostradamus has enjoyed an afterlife.

In life, he painstakingly manufactured a literary chaos that would turn the cloudy quatrains and half-page-long sentences of his prophetic prose narratives into a *tabula rasa* upon which each generation of interpreters could project their hopes, fears, and expectations. Moreover, for centuries now, biographers, blind believers, debunkers, and "prophegandists" have helped it along, with accurate and inaccurate dissemination of his prophetic legacy.

In the process the man and his life has all but disappeared in the giant shadow cast by his own controversial prophecies.

So just who was Nostradamus?

The new millennium and the "9/11" attacks have sparked the greatest debate yet about the efficacy of this man and his prophecies. There could be no better time to release a book that reassesses what we know about Nostradamus, the man.

The present book is the first complete and full-bodied biography and historical reassessment in over sixty years. This publication celebrates the 500-year anniversary of the birth of history's most famous and controversial prophet.

ABOUT THE AUTHOR

John Hogue is author of over 1,000 articles and 46 published books (1,180,000 copies sold) spanning 20 languages. He has predicted the winner of every US Presidential Election by popular vote since 1968, giving him a remarkable 13 and 0 batting average. He is considered a world-renowned authority on Nostradamus and the prophetic traditions of the world. He considers himself a "Rogue" scholar because he focuses on interpreting the world's ancient-to-modern prophets and prophecies with fresh eyes, seeking to connect readers with the shared and collective visions of terror, wonder and revelation about the future in a conversational narrative style. Hogue says the future is a temporal echo of actions initiated today. He strives to take readers "back to the present" empowering them to create a better destiny through accessing the untapped potentials of free will and meditation. Hogue currently lives on a picturesque island in the Pacific Northwest about an hour's drive and ferry ride north of Seattle, Washington.

Please visit him at www.hogueprophecy.com